POSTCARDS
from the EDGE

IAN COFFEY

POSTCARDS from the EDGE

FINDING GOD IN HARD PLACES

ivp

INTER-VARSITY PRESS
Norton Street, Nottingham NG7 3HR, England
Email: ivp@ivpbooks.com
Website: www.ivpbooks.com

First publised 2015

British Library Cataloguing in Publication Data
A catalogue record for this book is available from the British Library.

ISBN: 978-1-78359-205-0

Set in Dante 12/15pt
Typeset in Great Britain by CRB Associates, Potterhanworth, Lincolnshire
Printed in Great Britain by Ashford Colour Press Ltd, Gosport, Hampshire

*Inter-Varsity Press publishes Christian books that are true to the Bible and that
communicate the gospel, develop discipleship and strengthen the church for its mission in
the world.*

*Inter-Varsity Press is closely linked with the Universities and Colleges Christian
Fellowship, a student movement connecting Christian Unions in universities and colleges
throughout Great Britain, and a member movement of the International Fellowship of
Evangelical Students. Website: www.uccf.org.uk*

In memory of Rick Cole (1990–2015)
who ran fast and finished well

CONTENTS

ACKNOWLEDGMENTS

I have lived with this book for quite a few years.

It began life as I puzzled over various characters in the Bible who faced big challenges in their faith journeys. As a pastor and preacher, I thought it important to discover how they discovered God's grace in their time of need.

My work called me to serve people with similar struggles to those men and women in the Bible who found God in hard places. In turn, my personal study became the theme of various sermons and, like most communicators, I was interested in how these seemed to resonate with people and help them.

It was then I began the slow process of writing the chapters that make up this book. My publishers have been more than patient, and my gracious editor at IVP, Sam Parkinson, deserves some kind of award for perseverance.

Congregations as far apart as Australia, the Cayman Islands, the Republic of Ireland, the north of Scotland and the historic Keswick Convention in England have helped road-test the material, and helpful feedback has shaped the final text. I am grateful to these various congregations and to the men and women who give themselves to organizing events where proper place is given to both God's Word and the Holy Spirit.

There are places in these chapters where Scripture is silent, and we can only speculate as to exactly what took place. I have tried to make this clear where appropriate and encourage readers to come to their own view.

My wife Ruth was aptly named after Ruth in the Bible, whose postcard features in this book. She exemplifies all the qualities of her illustrious predecessor, and I am grateful for her consistent love and encouragement. We are a team ministry in every sense.

This book is dedicated to the memory of Rick Cole, a former student of our college who became a friend and colleague. This book was in its final stages of editing when Rick unexpectedly died at the age of twenty-four. He was a faithful follower of Jesus Christ who ran the race well and beat the rest of us to the finish line.

Rick's sudden death gave this book a fresh focus and a reminder that, in the hardest of places, God can be found.

Ian Coffey
Moorlands College
Lent 2015

INTRODUCTION

In my living room there hangs in pride of place a dark-brown frame. It contains three items:

- a black and white photo
- a crumbled letter
- a postcard.

All three are connected to a man I never met – my grand-father, Thomas Coffey.

The photo is of his grave, close to the Belgian battlefield where he died on 12 July 1916. The letter was the last he wrote home to his wife, Ada, just a few weeks before he was killed. The postcard is dated a few months earlier and was standard issue to the troops. It bears a drawing of a soldier dressed for the trenches, writing the card balanced on top of an upturned box. It contains the following lines:

In memory of the days gone by
Although we're now apart
I send this postcard just to show
You live within my heart

The three reminders are all we have of my grandfather. They came to light when clearing through my father's papers after his death. They were special to him as a link to his own father, whom he never knew, as, like tens of thousands of children, his father didn't return from the war that was meant to end all wars.

The letter and card were written in pencil. Tom thanks Ada for the photo she had sent of baby Arthur (my dad) and asks for pairs of socks, as he'd been issued with boots that were too big for him. He signs himself as 'your loving husband' and adds the poignant PS: 'Please excuse writing as I am writing this standing up.'

A postcard and a letter from the edge filled with special meaning for my family and me.

This book is along the same lines, as it looks at some people who found God in hard places. Their stories are contained in the pages of the Bible, and they remind us that in every age, people have faced challenges and difficulties. These men and women of faith discovered strength beyond themselves by relying on God, and they have left behind a legacy that lingers.

The Christian leader Paul wrote to the community of Christ's followers in Rome, reminding them:

> For everything that was written in the past was written to teach us, so that through the endurance taught in the Scriptures and the encouragement they provide we might have hope.
> (Romans 15:4)

Three key words in that statement sum up the purpose of this book: *endurance*, *encouragement* and *hope*. I pray that these postcards, written from the front line, will bring you all three.

USING THIS BOOK

Each chapter is divided into sections as follows:

Setting the scene

The chapter begins with a life story that illustrates the issue we are looking at.

Listening to the story

Some verses that give an account of a biblical character are explored and explained. It's recommended that you look up the verses mentioned and read them for yourself.

Learning from the story

This section sets out to apply lessons that we can learn from the examples set by these men and women of faith.

So what?

This contains several questions to help you think through some of the issues raised by the chapter. If you are studying this book as part of a group, these questions may offer a framework for discussion. If you are reading it alone, then it will help link to your personal situation.

Someone's story

Each postcard ends with a story that illustrates an important aspect of the chapter.

1. RUTH AND LOSS

Setting the scene

Let me introduce Ben and Emily Tanton, two students who met, fell in love and married at the college where I teach.

Ben was a member of my tutor group, and we got to know each other well outside the lecture room. One day he asked how he should go about asking Emily's father for permission to marry her. We talked it through, and I did my best to pass on some fatherly advice. (This included a strong suggestion that hiding the engagement ring in his sock drawer was not a wise move.) A few weeks into the vacation, I received an excited text from Ben. It had all gone to plan, and now he could move to the next stage: the proposal.

Fortunately, Emily said yes.

My wife Ruth and I led some marriage preparation classes and saw great potential in this young couple, who were sold out to God. Hospitality was part of their calling, and we talked about ways in which an open home and an open table can often lead to an open heart. They were up for whatever the Lord had in store.

We were sad when, in the summer of 2011, they graduated, but so glad that they found a post as youth leaders in a thriving church in the West Midlands. As the months passed, the news we received from Ben and Emily was positive. Inevitably there were a few challenges in settling to ministry in the real world, but they loved what they were doing and had begun to see solid fruit with the young people they served.

One Saturday in October, just one year into their work, and after a wonderful day off, Emily told Ben how happy she felt. More than that, she added how blessed she was to be serving the Lord she loved, doing a job she loved with the man she loved. Life could not be better for Emily as she went to sleep that night.

The next morning she died.

Getting ready for a busy Sunday at church, Emily collapsed in the bathroom. Despite much effort she never regained consciousness.

She was twenty-four years of age. Bright, articulate, passionate, funny, warm, caring, sensitive, enthusiastic, creative, dedicated. A few days after her death, Ben found a piece of artwork she had downloaded. Six stark words on a plain background: 'It is well with my soul.'

I have not been to a thanksgiving service quite like the one held for Emily, where laughter and tears were equally at home. Ben spoke with a quiet confidence, paying tribute to his young wife and testifying to God's strength shown through the care of God's people. At the front of the church stood a table with some of Emily's treasured things, each making a personal statement about her journey and the woman she had become: photographs, a dress, a favourite handbag.

At the centre of the table lay a scroll bound with a ribbon. It was the one presented to all our graduates; these scrolls contain the words of a charge read to them at their final service at college. It's all about serving Jesus well, running the race with courage, keeping going when it's hard and reaching out for the prize for those who cross the line.

But when Emily was presented with her scroll in June 2011, none of us realized how close she was to the end of her race.

Ben continues his race courageously, learning to live with loss, but trusting utterly in Jesus the Death-beater, who said,

> I am the resurrection and the life. He who believes in me will live, even though they die; and whoever lives by believing in me will never die.
> (John 11:25–26)

Listening to the story – Ruth 1:1–22

The book of Ruth is an extraordinary piece of writing, and one of the world's greatest love stories. It can be read in twenty minutes and plays out at various levels. It is a love story about a man and a woman from different ethnic backgrounds, but at the same time it tells us of a God who cares and provides. It deals with some big themes relating to women, as Carolyn Custis James writes,

> Widowhood and marriage, barrenness and childbirth, single parenting, loss of a child, the care-giver, male/female relationships all come up.[1]

And in the Big Story of God's rescue plan for lost humanity, the book of Ruth plays an important part in preparing for the coming of Jesus.

Some years ago, the author Warren Wiersbe wrote a short devotional based on the book of Ruth. He offered an overview of each of the four chapters, describing the unfolding story as Chapter 1 – *Weeping*, Chapter 2 – *Working*, Chapter 3 – *Waiting* and Chapter 4 – *Wedding*.[2]

We'll follow these useful signposts.

Chapter 1 – Weeping

Tragically, we are all too familiar with images of refugees, fleeing disaster with their meagre possessions, trudging on, hoping for a better, safer future. The story of Ruth starts with a refugee family looking for food in a time of famine. Elimelech, Naomi and their two sons, Mahlon and Kilion, left their home town of Bethlehem during a famine, and travelled in search of a better life in neighbouring Moab. The writer of the book goes out of their way to show that the problem was greater than a lack of food. 'In the days when the judges ruled . . .' (Ruth 1:1) refers to a largely dark period in Israel's history. This period between 1400 and 1000 BC was marked by what has been described as the 'Judges Cycle'. Israel turned its back on Yahweh and embraced idol worship, which provoked God's judgment. This led to military defeats, oppression by enemies and famine. The people repented and called out to God, and he raised up a judge as a deliverer; yet within a short space of time, the people forgot Yahweh and returned to their sinful ways, and the cycle was repeated. This depressing time is summed up by the last words in the book of Judges (see 21:25).

The family's situation took a turn for the worse when Elimelech died, leaving Naomi a widow. The two sons took Moabite brides, Orpah and Ruth, but tragedy struck again – twice over. First, despite a decade passing, neither woman conceived – and then Mahlon and Kilion died. We are not given the details, but the stark reality of Naomi's dilemma has been well described:

> The light had gone out in the Elimelech household –
> extinguished on Naomi's watch. Annihilation was a fate
> the Ancients feared most. The deaths of Mahlon and Kilion
> bereaved Naomi of her beloved children, wiped out her life's
> work as a woman, and brought the curtain down with a
> merciless thud on the future. When they buried Naomi's
> sons, they were essentially burying Naomi too.
>
> Overnight, her already diminished social status hit rock
> bottom, and Naomi was suddenly at risk. Without a male
> connection, she had no place in society and no source of
> income. Without a male protector, she was fair game for
> the unscrupulous who regularly preyed on helpless widows.
> Alone in a male-dominated world, Naomi was cast on the
> mercy of a society that had little interest in her.[3]

Loss comes in various forms, but it always carries the same expensive price tag. Suffering, it has been said, is 'wanting what you don't have and having what you don't want'.

Naomi takes the only option open to her and decides to return to Bethlehem. But she wants to release her daughters-in-law from any responsibility for her ongoing care, and she urges them to go back to their families. Maybe they can remarry and look forward to the prospect of having children. Life is so dark for Naomi that she believes that God's hand is against her, and she doesn't want her daughters-in-law to suffer with her any more.[4]

Orpah accepts this advice and kisses her mother-in-law goodbye. But Ruth won't budge. Something more than stubbornness lies behind her words. It is faith, raw and unrelenting:

Do not pressure me to desert you, to give up following you.
For where you go, I will go too; and where you lodge, I will
lodge too. Your people will be my people, and your God
will be my God.

Where you die I will die, and there I will be buried. Thus
may Yahweh do to me and more so if even death itself
separates me from you.[5]

Such loyalty is astonishing when we consider that Ruth
chooses an uncertain future over the opportunity to return to
the love of her family. But, it seems, her selfless act does little
to comfort Naomi. On returning home, Naomi changes her
name and announces that everything that has gone wrong in
her life is God's fault. He is the one to blame. The name
Naomi means 'pleasant', but from now on she wants to be
called Mara, which means 'bitter'. Her stark explanation says
much: 'I went away full, but the LORD has brought me back
empty' (Ruth 1:21).

Chapter 2 – Working

One of the main themes of this little book is that God is
working, even when we think nothing is happening. We are
introduced to Boaz, a relative of Elimelech, and a man of
wealth and influence. He is also someone whose faith touched
the whole of his life, even to the extent that he greeted his
workers in the name of Yahweh (Ruth 2:4). John Piper is not
alone is seeing the significance of this:

If you want to know a man's relation to God, it helps to find
out how far God has saturated him down to the details of
his everyday life. Evidently Boaz was such a God-saturated
man that his farming business and his relationship to his
employees was shot through with God. He greeted them

with God. And we will see that these were more than just pious platitudes.[6]

Ruth sets to work in his fields, not as a hired hand, but as a gleaner picking up handfuls of grain left by the harvesters. This was an established custom in Israel, to leave the pickings for the poor, as God had commanded in the law (Leviticus 19:9; 23:22; Deuteronomy 24:19). When Boaz discovers who she is, he orders that Ruth be treated kindly. When she thanks him for his kindness, he tells her he has heard about her compassion towards Naomi and the selfless choice she has made. He blesses her with words that will prove prophetic:

> May Yahweh repay your action, and may your wages be paid in full from Yahweh, the God of Israel, under whose wings you have come to seek refuge.[7]

When Ruth arrives home with armfuls of grain and explains this landowner's extraordinary generosity, Naomi asks his name. When she learns that it is Boaz, she reveals he is a close relative – a discovery that offers Naomi a glimmer of hope that God may not have abandoned her.

Chapter 3 – Waiting
Naomi devises a plan that will secure the continuation of her family line and provide security for both Ruth and herself. To Western readers, the account seems confusing and morally dubious at first sight. Others have done an excellent job at explaining the rich symbolism of ritual in Ruth's approach.[8]

Startled to find Ruth lying at his feet in the middle of the night – this of course being Naomi's plan – Boaz asks what is going on. She replies, 'Spread the corner of your garment over me, since you are a guardian-redeemer' (Ruth 3:9). It was the duty of the nearest male relative to marry a widow and keep the family line and inheritance intact (see Deuteronomy 25:5–10). This was an invitation to marriage, an imparting of information that he was one of the family members who could legally offer her protection, and a clever play on words. Boaz's earlier blessing spoke of her seeking refuge under Yahweh's wings, and Ruth uses the same word when inviting him to spread the corners (literally 'wings') of his cloak over her. She was offering him an opportunity to become the answer to his own prayer for her.

Boaz informs Ruth that there is one other male relative who can perform the task required under the Law of Moses.[9] He promises to resolve the matter and, ever the practical man, sends Ruth back to Naomi, once again laden with grain. The two women wait anxiously for news of the outcome.

Chapter 4 – Wedding

The story is moving to its climax, but not without an agonizing twist in the tale. Boaz approaches the man entitled to act as kinsman-redeemer. He tells this man of a piece of land Naomi wishes to sell (possibly her last sellable asset). The man immediately shows an interest (which is not what the reader of the story wants. The happy ending is melting . . .). However, Boaz points to the clause that proves to be the deal-breaker. The man who buys the land must marry the widow in order to maintain the dead man's family line. The relative turns down the offer (phew!), and Boaz is free to seal the deal.

Retrace the lines of this story and recall the dark grief that surrounded Naomi and Ruth. Naomi was a mother who lost her husband and two sons, feeling abandoned by God and left with no hope for the future. Ruth was a daughter-in-law who had been widowed young and was living as an alien in a foreign land with no-one to plead her cause. The two women faced a future as bleak and uncertain as we can imagine.

Then came this extraordinary, unexpected twist in the tale.

A wedding, the birth of a baby and Naomi experiencing the joy of cuddling her grandson draw this wonderful story to a close.

Well, almost.

The book concludes with a genealogy, the sort we are tempted to skim-read. But look carefully and you will see that the little lad on Naomi's knee turns out to be the granddad of King David, which in turn makes Ruth his great-grandma.

Yet Ruth was a foreigner. And that seems to make an important point.

Matthew, at the start of his Gospel, lists the genealogy of Jesus and includes five women who were 'outsiders' and not part of God's chosen people, Israel. It would be fair to say that each had a life that was tarnished in some way.

This appears deliberate, to underline the astounding truth that Jesus is for all.

Although Jesus was Jewish, his significance is not confined or limited to Jewish people but embraces all people in all places. Although there is of necessity a particularity about the identity of Jesus, it is a particularity for the sake of a universality. Jesus assumes a particular identity not in order to show that that identity is superior to anybody else's, but in order that he might sanctify and dignify the particular identities in which all human beings participate. The life and mission of Jesus are lived out for the sake of the whole human race.[10]

Learning from the story

But what about those struggling with loss who don't find the happy ending? For most who have experienced the searing pain of bereavement, it is just that – a burning hurt that won't go away.

Many who walk that lonely path would agree that 'Grief tears a hole in the fabric of life; we spend the rest of our lives trying to mend it.'[11]

Ruth's story offers hope and encouragement for those seeking to mend such holes. We are going to look at three aspects in particular: focus, faith and future.

Focus

We don't know at what point Ruth took the decision to stay with Naomi and turn down the offer to return to her family. She may even have been influenced by some changes in her family's circumstances. But what we do know is that despite her loss, she is clear in her sense of focus when she tells Naomi she is staying with her, come what may.

People respond to loss in different ways, and because of this, the grieving process varies. There is no 'one size fits all' when it comes to coping with bereavement, and we would all benefit from developing our understanding of how to help those who grieve.[12]

Those who have lost loved ones talk about the need to focus on those who are still alive, particularly the ones who are struggling with their own grief. That focus can take different forms, such as spending time with family and friends, forcing yourself to join in with activities or take up a new interest. None of these things can ever replace the hole left by the one we loved, but they represent a few tools that can help us mend. As a pastor, I have noticed the need for people to talk about the one who has died. Looking at old photos and retelling stories of holidays and life experiences are important ways of honouring and celebrating people we love. They may not be present in flesh, but they remain real in the memory. There is a need for care and balance here. Focusing on the present is important (even if the capacity to think about the future is limited), but at the same time, talking about the past can be of great help.

Faith

The Christian author and speaker, Elisabeth Elliot, has been widowed twice. Her first husband, Jim Elliot, was martyred when she was just thirty. Her second husband, the theologian Addison Leitch, died after a few short years of marriage. As she mourned the loss of Dr Leitch, she found great comfort in the words of the Apostles' Creed. She used it to answer the question: 'What things have not changed, even though my husband has died?'[13]

This illustrates how personal faith can bring comfort and strength at a time of loss. Grieving is part of being human, and to deny or suppress it as being unspiritual is as daft as it is dangerous.[14] Paul wrote to some new believers who were confused about how to handle death. He makes this comment:

> Brothers and sisters, we do not want you to be uninformed about those who sleep in death, so that you do not grieve like the rest of mankind, who have no hope.
> (1 Thessalonians 4:13)

Paul suggests that there are two types of grieving: one with hope and the other without it. The hope that sustains is that Jesus has beaten death and that it is not the end, but the beginning of new life. It's true that attending church when someone you love has died can be difficult sometimes, especially if the building holds special memories. Specific songs or hymns can make you feel sad, and I have known people who have taken a long time to adjust even to walking through the doors of a church. But that is where the help of a caring church community can help. Phone calls and visits, invitations for meals and tending to practical tasks that need attention are just a few ways in which we can show those who grieve that they are not alone.

Ruth's story contains those warm words of commitment to God when she promises Naomi that she will never leave her. It includes a significant phrase, 'Your people will be my people and your God my God' (Ruth 1:16), which is surprising when we remember the bitterness towards God that Naomi seems to hold in her heart. But perhaps something of her husband's faith had spoken to Ruth, and in her own loss she had reached out to Yahweh, the God of Israel, and decided to reject the idol worship and superstitions of her own people. Ruth reminds us that grief can sometimes be part of the process that leads us to greater faith.

Future

We have a friend whose husband died young; I was asked to lead his funeral. Just before the service, I asked our friend how she was feeling. She replied, 'My life ends today.'

Perhaps it was friendship that helped her be so honest. It was a moment of despair as she looked into a future that seemed empty and shapeless. Years of nothing in particular stretched out ahead. It looked a long and lonely road.

But that was some years ago, and lots of things have happened which have given shape and texture to her life. No, she hasn't 'got over it', as some would heartlessly describe it. How can you ever get over losing someone through death?

But she bravely embraces the future a day at a time (some days worse than others), and looks for what God has in store.

The late Queen Mother lived as a widow for many years. A close friend's husband died, and his widow asked her a searching question: 'Does it get any better?' The Queen Mother gave an honest reply that came with experience. 'No. But you get better at dealing with it.'[15]

Ruth embraced her future probably thinking that she would glean fields with other poor people for the rest of her days. She understood that Naomi would die one day and that she would probably be left alone. There was no pension waiting, but she trusted her future to God and then watched that future unfold in ways she could not have imagined.

Ruth leaves a legacy for those of us living with loss.

So what?

- Have you experienced loss? What helped you most at the time?
- What did you learn about helping others with their grief?
- What stands out about Ruth's character?
- Can you identify with Naomi's anger towards God?
- What would you say to someone who feels the same way as Naomi did?
- Boaz showed extraordinary kindness – is there someone you know who is in need of that sort of kindness? How can you provide it?

Jill's story

Jill Farwell saw two of her children die from a rare metabolic disease. The disease doesn't show until the child is about three, and, by the time their first child, Katie, was diagnosed, they already had their second child, Tom, who also had the syndrome. Katie died aged eleven, and Tom survived until he was fifteen. Jill and her husband Eddie nursed their children to the end and, out of their personal pain of loss, something beautiful was born.

I met Jill when she invited me to speak at a special service for the organization that she and Eddie had founded: the South West Children's Hospice. We met to plan the event, and Jill told me her story of loss. At one really dark time in their journey with two terminally ill children, she had woken Eddie in the middle of the night and exclaimed, 'We are going to take all this pain and do something good with it!'

And they did. Today there are three children's hospices serving the South West of England. In 1995, Little Bridge House was the first to open in Barnstaple, Devon. This was followed by Charlton Farm, near Bristol, in 2007 and the Little Harbour in St Austell, Cornwall, which opened in 2011.[16]

Millions of pounds were raised by a couple who didn't like public speaking, and scores of families have been helped as their dying children have received love and care in their last months on earth.

Taking pain and doing something good with it. It sounds like a good way to deal with loss.

2. ELIJAH AND DESPAIR

Setting the scene

David loved teaching. David loved children. Most of all, he loved teaching children. Since he had been seven years old, he had wanted to be a teacher and had never taken his eye off that goal.

Glancing at his CV, you'll see a man who has climbed the career ladder quickly and with seeming ease. He was a gifted communicator and a good organizer with strong emotional intelligence, and it was no surprise to see him achieve a headship by the age of thirty.

David did well, and after a few years he was asked to take on a failing school where special measures were in place. He turned the school around with some shrewd staff appointments and through monumental changes in the culture. The place that parents had avoided became the school that they wanted their kids to attend. The success story made the national press, and he became a well-known figure in television and radio studios when education was the topic under discussion. The Education Secretary famously referred to him in the House of Commons as 'a man who can' – and the tribute stuck. David was seen as a high achiever who turned failure into success, big-time.

But this had come at considerable cost. His marriage and family life had suffered, and his wife, Emma, would not easily describe her husband as a 'man who can', since she'd taken more than her share of responsibilities in caring for their two children and generally running the family. In his more reflective moments, David would acknowledge that his professional success carried a heavy price tag. Expensive holidays in the sun were not much compensation for two boys who badly needed a dad around more and for a partner who increasingly felt like a single parent.

Despite this, David's roller-coaster ride continued with the publication of his first book and a diary bursting with lectures, speaking engagements and social events.

Then, one Tuesday morning, he had a meeting that changed everything.

David didn't see what was coming and was unprepared for the shock. The appointment in his diary told him that the woman was a teaching union representative and next to the entry, David's PA had noted the name of a junior staff member. He was aware that this teacher had been unhappy for some time, but was being dealt with by one of his deputies. David had missed a number of management meetings recently and was way behind on his paperwork. The result was that he was not up to speed with all that had gone on and, although a file with detailed notes lay on his desk, he hadn't had time to look at it.

As he later described it, he felt as though he was facing Goliath without the benefit of a catapult.

The union rep was formidable and articulate. She cited dates, times and meetings without glancing at her notes. The substance of her case was clear: the staff member had been bullied persistently for months and her health had seriously deteriorated, as a doctor's report confirmed. Failure of process, abandonment of a duty of care, breach of professional standards – the list went on and on. This was institutional failure of the highest order, and the trail led to the desk of the head teacher. David's usually powerful persuasive skills failed to come to the rescue on this occasion, and he quickly realized that he and the school didn't have a leg to stand on. This case would go all the way to an industrial tribunal, and the resulting publicity would dash all the good work that he had done. The implications were enormous.

When the woman left his office, he called an emergency meeting of the Senior Management Team, which was followed by an uncomfortable telephone call to his Chair of Governors.

David drove the long way round that evening, stopping by the lake in a country park some miles from his house. He was as low as he'd ever felt in his life. All the achievements of recent years had evaporated like steam from a kettle. He felt alone, empty, afraid and a total failure.

The word 'despair' means to lose or give up hope.

And that was the place David found himself that Tuesday evening.

Listening to the story – 1 Kings 19:1–18

Elijah lived at a time when the spiritual tide of Israel was a long way out. King Ahab came to the throne in 874 BC and ruled for twenty-two years. He followed several other kings who were an unsavoury bunch, yet he topped them all, for as the Bible records, he 'did more evil in the eyes of the LORD than any of those before him' (1 Kings 16:30).

Ahab married Jezebel, daughter of the King of Sidon, in a shrewd political move that sealed a deal with the Phoenicians and gave unhindered access to an important Mediterranean port from which ships served the known world. Jezebel was a passionate evangelist for her father's religion – Baal worship. She persuaded Ahab to build a temple dedicated to Baal and to join her in regular ceremonies held there. In addition, she imported a teaching team numbering 450 prophets of Baal, plus an additional 400 prophets who served the goddess Asherah. As if that were not enough, she launched a campaign to murder the prophets of Yahweh, prompting many of them to go into hiding. Jezebel was a woman on a mission to convert a nation. And by all standards, she succeeded.

She had history on her side, as Baal worship went back hundreds of years and was rooted in the soil of the land. When the nation of Israel had entered the promised land of Canaan, they had found that the people living there were well established in worshipping Baal, the god of storm and fertility, who blessed the soil with fruitfulness.[1] When the question was asked, 'Where do the bumper harvests, olive oil and abundance of wine come from?', the answer was Baal. One writer sums up the intoxicating relevance of keeping favour with such a god:

> What could be more relevant to the life of any Canaanite farmer anxious over his wheat crop and cattle shed? When Baal was in top form, the world was pregnant with life. Here was a faith that suitably scratched where folks existentially itched. Finally, Baalism packed an appeal to sensuality. Sexual rites were built into the liturgy. Baal allowed you to serve him with all your glands. What did it matter if one's marriage was

rotten, one's wife uninteresting, one's life generally dull? There was always a 'holy' whore to be had at the Baal shrine. Perhaps such considerations can help us appreciate how Baalism could fascinate and charm.[2]

Baalism was, quite literally, a seductive faith.

Elijah was called to serve Yahweh at a difficult time and, by so doing, he placed his life in grave danger.

Elijah appears on this dark scene with no fanfare or introduction. His name was an in-your-face declaration of faith (it means 'Yahweh is My God'), and his message to King Ahab was a downright challenge to Baal's potency. Elijah announces that there will be no rain or dew until he (as Yahweh's agent) says so. Now Baal was seen as the storm god who directed the rain and caused crops to grow, but Yahweh was about to show that he was the one who could turn the taps on – or off (1 Kings 17:1). For over three years, the rain stopped and the nation began to suffer the consequences of severe drought. Elijah went into hiding and was miraculously preserved by God.[3]

Then Elijah summoned King Ahab and the whole nation to a spiritual showdown on Mount Carmel. In one of the most drama-filled chapters in the Old Testament, we read details of Elijah's bold challenge. It was a contest to see which was the real God, summed up in Elijah's defiant question: 'How long will you waver between two opinions? If the LORD is God, follow him; but if Baal is God, follow him' (1 Kings 18:21).[4]

The title fight centred on which God could answer by fire, setting his sacrifice alight. In the blue corner were 450 prophets of Baal, with their freshly slaughtered bull laid out on the altar. They prayed, shouted and danced, imploring Baal to answer with fire and ignite the carcass, but after hours of pleading, there was no answer. They worked themselves up into a frenzy, even cutting themselves until their blood flowed, to show the extent of their desperation.

Attention now turned to the red corner and the solitary figure of Elijah. He rebuilt the broken altar of Yahweh and laid the slaughtered bull on it. He dug a trench around the altar and ordered water to be poured on the carcass three times until it was thoroughly drenched. Elijah wanted there to be no doubt that what was about to happen was an act of God. The flooding of the offering and the wood underneath it would make it impossible to light. In complete contrast to the frantic antics of Baal's prophets, Elijah uttered a simple prayer to Yahweh, the covenant-keeping God. Scripture records, 'Then the fire of the LORD fell and burned up the sacrifice, the wood, the stones and the soil, and also licked up the water in the trench' (1 Kings 18:38).

The astonished crowd fell to their knees, declaring, 'Yahweh is God! Yahweh is God!' Elijah ordered the execution of the prophets of Baal before climbing back to the summit of Carmel. The fire had fallen, but now it was time for the rain to do the same. Elijah knelt, and prayed and prayed until the sky grew dark and the first drops of rain began to fall. After three and a half years of drought came the longed-for deluge and the sign of Yahweh's favour.

What happened next has been a source of surprise and discussion for centuries. King Ahab reported to Queen Jezebel all that had taken place, and she sent a personal messenger to Elijah with a death threat. The prophet who had been bold enough to take on a whole nation suddenly broke and ran for his life (1 Kings 19:1–3).

How could Elijah move from the triumph of Carmel to become a fleeing fugitive? What happened to the courageous prophet who had stood up against an army of pagan priests, but who now runs for his life at the threat of a queen whose hold on power was slipping fast? How did Elijah move from triumph to despair in just a few short hours?

Learning from the story

There are several lessons wrapped up in this incident that offer a few clues as to how we can sometimes find ourselves in the valley of despair. As the New Testament writer James reminds us, 'Elijah was a human being, even as we are . . .' (James 5:17).[5] But even more importantly, we see how the Lord dealt with his suffering servant and we gain insight into how our Heavenly Father meets us in those times of despair.

It appears that Elijah hit a perfect storm through a collision of circumstances that came together the morning after the triumph on Carmel. Over the years, people have speculated about the stark contrast between the astonishing display of courage from Elijah and, just hours later, his panic and despair.

The biblical account is factual. He travelled 100 miles south to Beersheba in Judah (out of Ahab and Jezebel's jurisdiction); he left his servant there and travelled a day's journey (perhaps twenty miles?) into the wilderness. Here he prays a desperate prayer that he might die, as he feels a total failure. Then he collapses into the sleep of exhaustion. Food is miraculously provided, followed by more sleep and a second meal. He then makes a 200-mile journey to Horeb, the mountain of God.

What is not so clear is what sparked this extraordinary journey. The Bible records that Elijah was afraid and ran for his life, because he took seriously Jezebel's sworn oath to kill him.[6] But what hit this man of God hard and caused him to lose hope and surrender to despair? We can't be certain, but I would suggest there were four interlinked factors that played their part in Elijah's panic attack.

Physically, Elijah was exhausted

Elijah was no wimp. He had managed to outrun the king's chariot the day before (1 Kings 18:46) by the power of Yahweh coming on him. He was a strong man morally, spiritually and physically. But we all have limits, and Elijah was no exception. Perhaps you can recall times when you have felt physically drained and unable to do another thing? Often this follows a time of stress, extra exertion or involvement in some big event that has taken everything out of us. Carmel had been a massive challenge and, the morning after the night before, Elijah was picking up the tab.

Mentally, Elijah was drained

We can't begin to imagine the impact of the previous few years on Elijah. He had lived as a fugitive on the run from a king who had vowed to kill him. He had been identified as a terrorist who had attacked his own people ('you troubler of Israel', 1 Kings 18:17) – and Ahab was not alone in that opinion. Elijah would not have won a popularity poll in Israel after months of drought. Then there was the mental strain of the Carmel event itself, when he stood alone against the hostile servants of Baal. The build-up of these pressures would have taken its toll on his tired mind. Perhaps you can identify with this kind of strain which can produce a state of exhaustion?

Emotionally, Elijah was spent

Most cars have a warning light to indicate when the fuel is close to running out. Some risk-takers choose to ignore it and try to take the car beyond the advised limit. More fool them if the car stops when it's pouring with rain and the nearest garage is miles away! Emotionally, Elijah had been running on empty for three and a half years. Fed by ravens in Kerith

Brook, then hiding as a guest of a widow in the foreign town of Zarephath, Elijah had lived with insecurity. Then there was the trauma of the widow's only son dying suddenly and Elijah intervening to bring the lad back to life (1 Kings 17). All these things carried an emotional cost, and the day after Carmel, there was nothing left in the tank.

Spiritually, Elijah was under attack

Baal worship was demonic,[7] and Elijah's bold stand against it prompted a spiritual backlash from the forces of darkness. Elijah had taken enemy territory after all the people of Israel had publicly repented and declared their renewed allegiance to Yahweh in response to the contest on Carmel (1 Kings 18:39). He now found himself under direct spiritual attack as a consequence of this victory in the spiritual life of the nation of Israel.

I have described these factors as a 'perfect storm', as this seems the best way to describe how Elijah (whose courage, integrity and clear-sightedness are unquestioned) found himself swamped by the circumstances that surrounded him that particular day. The Bible tells us his response: 'Elijah was afraid and ran for his life' (1 Kings 19:3). His little boat was swamped by massive waves and he took the only course of action he could see. Elijah abandoned ship.

Bad decisions are like a line of dominoes. One knocks another and soon they all fall down. There was a sequence that followed Elijah's decision to listen to Jezebel's threat and run for his life. First, he gave way to fear, and then he forsook friendship by leaving his servant behind. His solitary journey took him deep into the desert, and his inner journey took him down the dark spiral staircase of despair. His desert steps matched his descent to the place of utter hopelessness. Taking shelter from the sun under a broom tree, he offered a prayer that was more of a cry of desperation: 'I have had enough, LORD . . . Take my life; I am no better than my ancestors' (1 Kings 19:4). Elijah felt a total failure and wanted to die. And as he closed his eyes and settled to rest in the shade of the broom tree, he hoped with all his heavy heart that God would answer his prayer.

Faced with a burnt-out prophet, what would you do? (That's a question suggested in the 'So what?' section later in this chapter.) Looking at how God dealt with Elijah helps us to understand why the Bible talks about the Lord's great love, never-failing compassion and consistent faithfulness (Lamentations 3:22–23).

The Lord met Elijah at every point of his need.

Physically, he gave his exhausted servant some much-needed rest. He let him sleep before an angel woke him with the offer of freshly baked bread and refreshing water. Then he allowed Elijah to sleep some more before the angelic visitor woke him a second time and encouraged him to eat more food. The next step in the plan was a six-week hiking holiday – and Elijah needed fuel for the journey (1 Kings 19:5–8).

Mentally, the forty days of walking to Horeb[8] provided an enforced break away from the spotlight and people pressures. This reminds us that recreation is about re-creation and that holidays and days off can and should be Sabbaths of rest.

Emotionally, this period was a time for Elijah to do some processing and allow everything to catch up. He needed to find order in his upside-down world again.

Spiritually, Horeb was an opportunity for a fresh revelation of God and a renewed commission to go back and serve. Much has been written and preached about the Horeb experience and the relevance of the wind, earthquake and fire (1 Kings 19:11–13). Why was God absent from these powerful phenomena and why did he choose instead to reveal himself in the 'gentle whisper'? I think the key to understanding is in the invitation: 'Go out and stand on the mountain in the presence of the LORD, for the LORD is about to pass by' (v. 11). Elijah understood about Yahweh, who controlled the elements of nature – Elijah's experience had taught him much about God's power. But the gentle whisper signalled a new understanding for this seasoned prophet. God is never limited in the ways he reveals himself. This was a new understanding for a man who had been drowning in despair. God was close enough that Elijah could hear the whisper and feel the breath against his face. On the summit of Horeb, the most high God revealed himself to Elijah as the most nigh God.[9]

Twice Elijah is asked the same question, 'What are you doing here?', and twice he gives the same answer, simply telling God what he already knew (a mistake regularly repeated in prayer meetings!). In response, the Lord issues a clear set of instructions for Elijah to carry out. There's no question of retirement; it's very much business as usual – but not before one small yet important correction is addressed. Elijah was convinced that he was the last man standing so far as loyalty to Yahweh was concerned. His despair had led to temporary amnesia, as he seemed to have forgotten faithful Obadiah and his courageous rescue mission (1 Kings 18:9–15). The Lord wanted to set the record straight; there were 7,000 faithful followers who had remained loyal to Yahweh, despite the cultural pressures to worship Baal. Heaven misses nothing, and Elijah needed to learn that lesson.

I come away from this story having learned three important lessons of my own.

1. How I view God

Elijah was not written off as a failure. But God met this brave servant at his various points of need. God deals with him with tenderness and compassion, which dispels any unhelpful images of a tyrannical dictator looking keenly to spot my failures and to reject me as a failure.

2. How I treat myself

I am a whole person and need to take responsibility for my physical, mental, emotional and spiritual well-being. There is nothing godly about burn-out.

3. How I handle times of despair

Elijah experienced despair, and I shouldn't be surprised if there are times when I face the same. God met Elijah in his darkest time, and I can trust God to do the same for me.

So what?

- Have you known a time of despair? What helped you through that time – and what was less than helpful?
- Elijah was hit by a 'perfect storm' – are there ways he could have avoided this?
- How would you have dealt with Elijah when he ran away?
- Do you ever catch yourself saying (or thinking), 'I'm the only one who . . .' (sometimes called the 'Elijah syndrome')? How can we avoid this?
- Elijah stood strong against the prevailing culture of Baal worship. Where do you need to stand strong?

Romans 8 Verse 1's story

In one of the churches where I served, we had a team member, Dawn, who visited Uganda one summer and shared in several weeks of ministry with various churches. Dawn arrived home and dropped by my office, full of stories about her various adventures. She had met some wonderful people, but one man stood out in her memory. 'He is one of the most gifted evangelists I've met,' she told me, and went on to detail some of the many lessons he'd taught her.

'What's his name?' I asked.

'Romans 8 verse 1,' was her reply.

'Dawn, that's a Bible reference, not a name!' I protested.

But she assured me that was his legal name, and went on to tell me the man's remarkable story.

He was born in a village and lived alone with his mother. When he was old enough to understand, he was told that his father had moved away long before and wouldn't be returning. As a boy, he loved to help the visiting priest who came every week to conduct services. He would help arrange things in the small chapel and make sure everything was to hand. One day he announced proudly, 'When I grow up, I will become a priest just like you.' His enthusiasm met with a stony silence. He persisted. 'Don't you think I can become a priest like you?' Then the bombshell fell. 'That will never happen,' the priest replied. 'You'll never become a priest – because you are a bastard!'

The words cut like a knife. Things were made worse when the boy asked his mother to tell him the truth about the real circumstances of his birth. He was devastated to realize that the silent shame his mother had lived with would now become the mantle he would share for the rest of his life.

As the boy grew into manhood, God, faith and church faded to black. He didn't count. There was simply no room for him within the community of God's people.

Feeling God-forsaken is the ultimate point of despair.

One day, a man came into his life with a different story. It was one of hope. It was the story of Jesus, who took on himself our sins and became God-forsaken on our behalf. The young man learned for the first time how the Son of God died on the cross to let outsiders become insiders.

The young man came into God's family as a result of that conversation and was baptized as a follower of Jesus. As is customary in some cultures, he was given a new name at baptism as a symbol of his changed life. And the name he was given was Romans 8 Verse 1, which reads:

> Therefore, there is now no condemnation for those who are in Christ Jesus.

A message of hope for any who despair.

PS. Things worked out well for David. He faced a difficult few months and eventually left his post, taking a job in another part of the country. He made a conscious decision to commit more time to his family. It has not been easy, but he and Emma are now in a better place.

3. ESTHER AND COURAGE

Setting the scene

Rick had worked for the same company since leaving school. He started on the shop floor of a small engineering business, and over thirty years or so had seen it grow larger than anyone could have predicted.

An entrepreneur had bought the business a few years after Rick started, and had led it into the global marketplace, where sales rocketed. The new owner liked Rick and took an interest in his development. As a result, Rick progressed through increasingly senior positions, eventually becoming Managing Director when he was still in his late thirties.

His boss, meanwhile, turned his attention to developing other businesses, confident that Rick was a safe pair of hands. His confidence proved true, as the company grew in size and reputation, even weathering some economic storms with great skill.

The company looked after its employees well, made frequent

contributions to local charities and had an excellent reputation among its customers.

Rick is a committed Christian who takes his faith seriously. A few summers back, he read a book about integrating your faith into the world of work. He found it helpful, although one chapter on ethical choices challenged him deeply. The author talked about maintaining clear boundaries between honest and dishonest practices. Rick knew some things in his company were in a grey area when it came to business practice.

On his return from holiday, Rick went to see his vicar, who had spent some years in business himself and understood how the world sometimes worked. In confidence, Rick explained his dilemma. His minister agreed with his assessment that what was happening could be interpreted as illegal. The two agreed a course of action that would involve Rick talking to the company owner and explaining his misgivings.

Rick faced the meeting with trepidation. He got on well with his boss generally, but he was a man with a commanding presence and a volatile temperament. Rick knew that this discussion could lead to an end of their working relationship, and he realized that looking for another job in his fifties would not be a great prospect.

But the meeting went better than expected. Rick explained his concerns and the boss listened carefully. After a few moments of quiet thought, his boss put a hand on the table and said, 'Rick, if you're not comfortable with us doing that, then let's stop doing it.'

The conversation switched to other matters.

That evening, Rick rang his minister to share the remarkable news. Rick thanked him for his prayers and advice, then added, 'As my boss got up to leave, he shook my hand and said, "Rick, never hold back on raising things that make you uncomfortable. You're a man of integrity – which is why I put you in the position you are in now." '

Not everyone has found a boss as sympathetic as that. Some have lost their jobs for speaking up and speaking out. But courage – the theme of this postcard – is about doing the right thing, whether it works for us or against us. Because doing the right thing is always the right thing to do.

Listening to the story – Esther 4:1–17

The book of Esther is unique for at least two reasons. First, it makes no mention of God, which seems quite strange for a Bible book; secondly, it is quite non-religious.[1] Despite these facts, God's fingerprints are all over the remarkable story, and a careful reading of Esther has brought strength and joy to people experiencing suffering.

It has special resonance for those living in a secular world that pushes God to the margins and tries to bury faith as a curiosity from a bygone age. Esther's story tells us that God is waiting in the wings, working his greater purpose, whether we can perceive it or not.

The book has not always been received and understood well. The early Church Fathers failed to write one commentary on Esther between them, and Martin Luther dismissed it for containing too much 'pagan naughtiness'!

For the Jewish community, Esther has special significance, as the story gave rise to one of the great annual Jewish festivals, Purim.[2] The book is read aloud during the two-day festival, which is a time of exuberance, eating, drinking and exchanging presents.

Four main characters
As with any story, there are key players as well as those

with bit parts. Here are the four main characters, in order of appearance.

King Xerxes

He rejoiced in the title 'The Great King, the King of Kings', and ruled as supreme head of the Persian Empire,[3] which spanned a vast part of the known world at that time. In modern-day terms, it covered Turkey, Iraq, Iran, Pakistan, Jordan, Lebanon, Israel and parts of Egypt, Sudan, Libya and Arabia. It was administered by a massive bureaucratic structure, and communication was via a 'pony express' system that dispatched official decrees across the Empire with remarkable speed and efficiency. Any edict sealed by the king was irrevocable.[4]

The book of Esther portrays him as an arrogant, foolish man; he led a self-centred life and made rash choices. The opening chapter tells of a lavish celebration hosted by Xerxes at his winter palace (Esther 1:1–8). The party ran for six months and was an ostentatious display of his wealth and power. His guest list included the power-brokers and leaders of the Empire, which has led historians to speculate that he was planning an extensive military campaign against his arch-enemies, the Greeks.

The climax of this festival was a seven-day feast where the wine flowed freely. On the final day, Xerxes sent for Queen Vashti, his consort, 'in order to display her beauty to the people and nobles, for she was lovely to look at' (Esther 1:11).

The royal summons didn't go down well – Vashti declined, which sparked a right royal row.[5] Xerxes was furious, and his advisers proved to be as stupid (and perhaps as drunk?) as their monarch. Determined to make a drama out of a crisis, they took the view that Vashti's defiance would spread a domestic forest fire across the Empire, as men's authority would be usurped. The thought of women revolting was too much to bear, and so a royal decree was issued that Vashti would never again enter the king's presence. In one swift act, she was both deposed and divorced.

The decision was posted across the Empire, and the writer of the book notes (perhaps with tongue in cheek) that the decree declared 'that every man should be ruler over his own household' (Esther 1:22). The sledgehammer had hit the nut.

A few years later, Xerxes, probably regretting his actions towards Vashti, was persuaded to seek a replacement.[6]

The royal advisers, ever ready to please, came up with a plan that involved an empire-wide beauty contest to select the best-looking unmarried women. They would be brought to the palace, subjected to intense beauty treatments and then the king would have the opportunity to spend a night with each in turn, before deciding who would be the new queen. This 'try before you buy' suggestion appealed to Xerxes, and the search began (Esther 2:2–4).

Mordecai

Mordecai's great-granddad had been taken into exile when Jerusalem had fallen, a century before, to King Nebuchadnezzar, ruler of the Babylonian Empire. His family had decided not to return to their homeland, when eventually Babylonian power crumbled; instead, they found a new life under Persian rule.[7] It seemed that Mordecai held a minor position within the royal household as an administrator. But as the writer introduces him, it is underlined that Mordecai was a Jew from the tribal clan of Benjamin (Esther 2:5).

Esther

The third main player is the woman who lends her name to the title of the book. Esther[8] was orphaned and taken in by her cousin Mordecai, who became a surrogate father.

It is said of her that she 'had a lovely figure and was beautiful' (Esther 2:7), and so she becomes caught up in the contest to find a replacement queen. She finds favour in the eyes of the royal attendant in charge of the process, but more significantly, she wins Xerxes' approval. We are told:

> Now the king was attracted to Esther more than to any of the other women, and she won his favour and approval more than any of the other virgins. So he set a royal crown on her head and made her queen instead of Vashti.
> (Esther 2:17)

At this point in the story, we are told two important pieces of information, the full impact of which will be seen later. First, Esther had been advised by Mordecai to keep her Jewish origins secret and let no-one know the details of her background.[9]

Secondly, we are told about a plot to assassinate Xerxes that Mordecai uncovers through accidentally overhearing a conversation between two conspirators. He gets word to Esther and the men are caught and executed. The Persian Civil Service, diligent as ever, note the king's lucky escape in the royal records. Mordecai is named as the one who uncovered the plot, but (significantly) he is not thanked or rewarded for his diligence and loyalty (Esther 2:21–23). This oversight will prove vitally important as the story unfolds.

Haman

Every good story has a villain, and Haman is well suited to the part. But he was no make-believe pantomime baddy; he was a cruel and dangerous man of the sort that continues to be a scourge in today's world. When the book of Esther is read aloud during the feast of Purim, Haman's name provokes an intense reaction in the congregation.

During the recitation of the book, it is customary to drown out Haman's name. At regular intervals the synagogue erupts like a sports stadium into a cacophony of drums, cymbals, trumpets, stomping feet and jeering. Old football rattles, long disappeared from the terraces, come in particularly handy: in fact, special Purim rattles (in Yiddish they are known as *greggers*) used to be made. In medieval times, children made effigies of Haman, hung them outside the synagogue and pelted them with missiles.[10]

It is reported that Jewish children enjoy Purim more than any other festival, possibly because it is a time for sharing food, sweets and presents. In addition, there are often fancy-dress and celebration parties. But I suspect the opportunity to make ear-splitting noise in the synagogue, with the aim of drowning out Haman's name, must be a big attraction. (His name is mentioned fifty-three times!)

What is behind this riotous tradition? The answer lies in his murderous plan to annihilate all Jews in the Empire. The phrase 'ethnic cleansing' was invented in the twentieth century, but its evil principles are as old as human history.

Haman is introduced as 'son of Hammedatha, the Agagite' (Esther 3:1); some biblical scholars believe that this hints at the root of his perverse hatred of the Jewish people. They make the connection with Agag, the Amalekite king, claiming Haman was a direct descendant of the Amalekites, historic enemies of the Jews.[11]

A terrible plan

Haman climbed the greasy pole of power and became Xerxes' most trusted adviser, receiving deference from all royal officials. But Mordecai refused to join in with this sycophancy that bordered on idolatry, and that sparked Haman's fury

(Esther 3:1ff.). Haman decided to get revenge not just on Mordecai, but on all Jewish people everywhere.

In a culture ruled by superstition, the timing of Haman's plan was left to the rolling of dice on a calendar and a specific date in eleven months' time.[12] Haman exercised his influence over King Xerxes so that the king issued a decree that on that day, Jews across the Empire should be killed and their property plundered. Those who carried out the slaughter would be free from prosecution. Shockwaves of despair spread as news of the impending disaster reached the farthest corners of the Empire.

Mordecai sends a message to Esther, urging her to speak to the king and plead for her people. She reports that Xerxes has not summoned her for a month, and that to enter his presence uninvited could cause her death.[13] In what is probably the best-known part of the story, Mordecai sends a stark reply:

> Do not think that because you are in the king's house you alone of all the Jews will escape. For if you remain silent at this time, relief and deliverance for the Jews will arise from another place, but you and your father's family will perish. And who knows but that you have come to your royal position for such a time as this?
> (Esther 4:13–14)

Esther urges Mordecai to get other Jews to join her in fasting for three days, and tells him she will then take the biggest step of faith and approach the king. And when she does . . .

I encourage you to read the text for yourself and see how the evil Haman was eventually exposed, the death threat to millions averted and the faithful Mordecai honoured.[14]

Learning from the story

People have pondered Esther's story for centuries, and seen within it a tapestry of truth enlightening our understanding of God's providence as well as his silence. But, for our current chapter, let's put the focus on Esther's remarkable act of courage.

We don't know the time-frame between the various messages that passed between Esther and Mordecai, or how long it took for her to consider his challenge to get involved. But from her reply and subsequent actions, we can see four statements of intent that lay behind her decision. They give us more than a clue about the process involved in taking brave and costly decisions.

1. 'I need to get involved'

Esther's decision to call for others to join her fast mark an important moment where she crossed over from being a spectator to becoming involved. It is like witnessing a car crash and answering the question: 'Do I stop and help or drive on by?'

Martin Niemöller was a German pastor, imprisoned by the Nazis for eight years for opposing Hitler. He was among a group of church leaders who drafted the Stuttgart Declaration of Guilt at the end of World War 2. It was a statement from the Evangelical Church in Germany that acknowledged their failure to speak out against the Third Reich. Part of it read:

> . . . we accuse ourselves for not standing to our beliefs more courageously, for not praying more faithfully, for not believing more joyously, and for not loving more ardently.[15]

In a famous poem, Niemöller expressed the consequences of keeping quiet instead of speaking out:

First they came for the communists,
and I didn't speak out because I wasn't a communist.
Then they came for the socialists,
and I didn't speak out because I wasn't a socialist.
Then they came for the trade unionists,
and I didn't speak out because I wasn't a trade unionist.
Then they came for me,
and there was no one left to speak for me.[16]

2. 'This is about a bigger cause'

Esther lived in the part of the king's palace reserved for wives and concubines. Such isolation could have led her to live in a bubble, unconcerned about anything beyond her immediate needs and duties.

Mordecai lifted her eyes to a broader horizon by telling her, 'If you don't act, relief and deliverance for the Jews will arise from another place.' Some see this as an allusion to God, while others think that Mordecai had human intervention in mind. Personally, I think Mordecai was a man of faith and his comment reflects his belief that Yahweh – the God of his fathers – would not stand idly by as his chosen people were threatened with annihilation. At this historical distance, we can't be certain, but we can see Esther connecting with the enormity of what was envisaged. She saw her people facing certain slaughter across the far reaches of the Empire, and realized that she was in the unique (yet dangerous) position of being able to change the script. All this played a significant part in bringing her to her personal tipping point.

3. 'My self-interest comes second'

Every so often, a lone individual stands up in a solitary act of protest and captures the imagination of millions. One such has become known simply as the 'Tank Man'. The *New York Times* reported that:

> ... on June 5, 1989, following weeks of huge protests in Beijing and a crackdown that resulted in the deaths of hundreds, a lone man stepped in front of a column of tanks rumbling past Tiananmen Square. The moment instantly became a symbol of the protests as well as a symbol against oppression worldwide – an anonymous act of defiance seared into our collective consciousnesses.[17]

Eyewitnesses report that the man, carrying his shopping bags, simply stood in the path of three tanks, with his hands raised in silent protest. Bundled away by security forces, his name and his fate are unknown. In China, images and reports of the incident are blocked on the internet, but his action is not forgotten and has inspired others to take similar stands of selfless defiance.

The urge for self-protection is a strong force, and, it would seem, the art of summoning courage involves embracing personal risk. For Esther to approach the king uninvited was risk with a capital R. Her life was on the line, and her action called for courage with a capital C.

4. 'I am not here by accident'

Once when I was visiting a famous art exhibition, an attendant asked me to step back from the painting I was viewing. I thought I had breached security regulations and apologized. 'No, sir,' the man replied, 'You are standing too close to get the full impact of the painting – stand back and see!' It wasn't security that bothered him, but my need to view the whole painting.

I am as guilty as anyone in having my nose pressed too close to the canvas. We all need to step back and view the bigger picture sometimes.

Mordecai invited Esther to reflect on all that had happened in her life to lead her to this point. Probably no-one else was close enough to put such a question to her. As her surrogate dad, he had shared much of the journey and had earned the right to ask, 'Why do you think you've been placed where you are?'

It's like the phrase chanted by crowds in the Romanian Revolution in December 1989, which led to the downfall of Communist dictator Nicolae Ceauşescu. Crowds took to the streets of Timişoara, shouting, 'If not now, when? If not us, who?'[18]

I am reminded of a parallel between Esther's situation and Joseph's confident assertion to his treacherous brothers: 'You intended to harm me, but God intended it for good to accomplish what is now being done, the saving of many lives' (Genesis 50:20). Joseph identified God's greater purpose at work in his personal circumstances. It wasn't luck that landed him the job as Egypt's prime minister, but God.

We may not reach elevated positions like Esther or Joseph, but we may well find ourselves in what could be described as significant places. I have written elsewhere about the importance of discovering a sense of vocation as disciples of Christ:

In the English language, we make a distinction between a *vocation* (which comes from a Latin word meaning *calling*) and a *job*. Unlike a paid job, which you might be doing just to pay the rent, a vocation means that there is a sense in which you have an ambition, a call, to go into that particular field of work. Now that's a very Christian idea: our vocation, our calling, is to live as disciples of Christ, although our actual jobs may change from time to time.[19]

When we look at our lives through the lens of vocation, we are able to take in the bigger picture and understand that God has placed us where we are for a purpose.

It may be that this chapter on courage strikes a chord with you because it is something that you feel you need right now. Perhaps you feel the need to be bold and step out in faith? Maybe the issue is one of speaking up and saying something that needs to be heard? It could be that you face the very real risk of failure and some personal cost. But, as the story of Esther reminds us, the need to do the right thing is paramount. And as people of faith, we are not abandoned. Because of Jesus, we are not alone. That is not a cliché, but a theological fact. Because he tasted aloneness – utter alienation from God – we don't need to. As Paul, the Christian leader, wrote, 'I can do all this through him who gives me strength' (Philippians 4:13).

So what?

- When do you need courage?
- What can we learn from Esther's story about living in a world where God seems absent?
- The book tells the history of the festival of Purim. As Christians, do we celebrate enough? And do we celebrate the right things?
- How can we identify a bigger cause that demands our involvement?
- Mordecai's encouragement to Esther played a key role in her story. What lessons can we draw from his example? Do we know people who need encouragement in their calling? How can we give this?
- What steps can you take to find strength?

Malala's story

Malala Yousafzai, a Pakistani schoolgirl, rose to prominence at the end of 2012 when she was shot by the Taliban for attending school and publicly asserting the right for girls to be educated. After undergoing lifesaving surgery, she and her family relocated to the UK.

On Friday 12 July 2013 – Malala's sixteenth birthday – she was invited to address the United Nations General Assembly in New York. It was dubbed Malala Day, in honour of her courage. Here is part of her address:

> Dear friends, on 9 October 2012, the Taliban shot me on the left side of my forehead. They shot my friends, too. They thought that the bullets would silence us, but they failed. And out of that silence came thousands of voices. The terrorists thought they would change my aims and stop my ambitions. But nothing changed in my life except this: weakness, fear and hopelessness died. Strength, power and courage was born. I am the same Malala. My ambitions are the same. My hopes are the same. And my dreams are the same. Dear sisters and brothers, I am not against anyone. Neither am I here to speak in terms of personal revenge against the Taliban or any other terrorist group. I am here to speak for the right of education for every child. I want education for the sons and daughters of the Taliban and all the terrorists and extremists. I do not even hate the Talib who shot me.[20]

Some years ago, I received a letter from a friend. The letter ended with some wise words I needed at the time and have returned to many times: 'If you're going to be brave, be very, very brave.'

4. JEREMIAH AND INADEQUACY

Setting the scene

Jo had a troubled childhood. Her parents split up when she was small, and her mother struggled to cope with her and two younger sisters. Money was tight and Mum had an alcohol addiction, which is where most of their money went. Eventually, Jo and her sisters were placed in care. That led to a succession of different children's homes, of foster families and the pain of separation.

She lost count of the schools she attended over the years and admits that her coping mechanism was to become aggressive and uncooperative with everyone, including the foster carers, social workers and teachers who tried their best to help a very troubled girl.

Jo's mum eventually found help for her drink problem and spent several months in rehab before making a fresh start. She found a new boyfriend who had a steady job, and was able to have Jo and her sisters live with her once more. But the years of separation had taken their toll. Jo was by now in her early teens and had established a pattern of behaviour that was almost impossible to manage. It would start with shouting and swearing, but would usually escalate to smashing things or physically attacking people who tried to calm her down.

The relationship between Jo and her mum was the usual trigger for these outbursts. The years apart had fuelled a volcano of anger deep inside Jo. She put the blame for her pain squarely on the shoulders of her mother. Because of her mum's drinking, Jo felt she had lost everything she cared about – most of all her relationship with her dad, who had lost touch with the family years before. In her angry outbursts, Jo would scream dreadful things to her mum – accusations that were often accompanied by physical blows.

Sadly, Jo's mum could give as good as she could get, and the two would shout themselves hoarse with abuse, slapping and hitting out at one another. The new boyfriend became adept at calming things down as he found himself an involuntary referee in these regular rows.

Fast forward a few decades. Jo is happily married and has two young sons. You wouldn't believe she was the same person as that angry teenager. Seven years ago, Jo was invited to attend an Alpha course at her local Anglican church. This led to her deciding to become a committed Christian. Her husband, Paul, made a similar commitment a year later. They are both involved in the church, and their boys are enthusiastic regulars in the children's programme.

In her adult life, Jo had a succession of jobs, until one enterprising boss encouraged her to take a day-release course which eventually led to her getting a place at university and going on to train and qualify as a teacher.

From the outside, Jo's life looks sorted. Despite a bleak start, she has made something of herself and has a family, a faith, a rewarding job and a great circle of friends. But on the inside, Jo is far from sorted. She struggles with a lack of self-worth and the fear that if people knew what she was really like, no-one would be her friend.

Jo's mum died some years ago, and although their relationship had improved considerably, they were never able to address the 'nightmare years', as her mum used to call them. Jo often replays in her head some of those violent rows and recalls the hurtful words. Her faith has helped her to understand forgiveness in a deeper way. She knows that she needs to forgive as well as to be forgiven. But there is so much about the past that she wishes she could change.

A recurring memory for Jo is her mum screaming at her, 'You are nothing and you'll amount to nothing. You're useless and just a waste of space!' That is the tape that often plays in her head when Jo is under pressure, and it has held her back in many areas of her life. She has turned down promotions at the school where she works, refused to apply for jobs she is well qualified for and hangs back from volunteering for anything she is invited to take part in at church.

Jo's bottom line is that she doesn't feel adequate, despite all the evidence that says otherwise. So she can identify with the subject of our next postcard from the edge. Jeremiah was called to do a job that he didn't think he could handle. His life offers several insights into how feelings of inadequacy can be faced and overcome.

Listening to the story – Jeremiah 1:1–19

Jeremiah's life, in one sentence, was that he was called at a difficult time to deliver an uncomfortable message and live in dangerous circumstances.

The Old Testament book that bears his name is long, complicated and, on one level, quite depressing. Two famous images capture something of this lonely prophet's reputation. Michelangelo's fresco in the Sistine Chapel[1] depicts a seated and sombre Jeremiah, resting his head in his right hand in response to the destruction of Jerusalem. Rembrandt's[2] portrayal also depicts the prophet with his head propped by his hand, again in a state of grief over the destruction of Jerusalem. With a book entitled Lamentations to his credit, we can understand why 'being a Jeremiah' entered the English language as a description of someone who is a wet blanket, and why a 'jeremiad' is the name given to a mournful poem or dirge.

But this is grossly unfair. Jeremiah's life deserves closer inspection, and what emerges is a picture of a man of faith, passionate for God's glory and willing to swim against the tide of his prevailing culture with both courage and stickability. Dismissed by his countrymen as a traitor, he was actually a patriot of the highest order. Consider this brief overview of his life and times.

The man

Jeremiah was born into an influential religious family who lived in Anathoth (Jeremiah 1:1), a few miles north of Jerusalem. It was one of a group of towns exclusively reserved for priests and their families. He was the nephew of Shallum, husband of Huldah the prophetess who foretold the destruction of Jerusalem (Jeremiah 32:7; 2 Kings 22:14ff.). Being so close to Jerusalem, Jeremiah lived at the centre of national life, and, with the influences of his priestly and prophetic family surrounding him, he was ideally positioned for the role that God called him to undertake.

Yet, strange as it may seem, his family were less than supportive – especially when his hard-hitting prophecies became public news. They plotted against him and challenged his words to the extent that he could no longer trust them (Jeremiah 11:21; 12:6). They had even threatened to kill Jeremiah if he did not stop preaching what they considered to be treacherous lies against his own nation.

His times

Jeremiah was born at a time of religious and political change. Tectonic plates of power were shifting as the Assyrian Empire that had dominated for two centuries began to disintegrate and the Babylonians and Egyptians vied to fill the vacuum. The Battle of Carchemish in 605 BC gave the Babylonians a decisive victory over the Egyptians and the remnant of the Assyrian army. Babylon was the new empire that would rule for several decades. What made Jeremiah so unpopular with his contemporaries was his assertion that these political changes were all part of God's greater purpose.[3] And that purpose – quite simply – was Yahweh's judgment against his rebellious, covenant-breaking people.

Within Jeremiah's home nation of Judah, it was a time of spiritual, moral and political crisis. He lived through the reigns of seven kings,[4] and his forty-year ministry coincided with five of them (two of them reigned for just twelve weeks each). Josiah[5] was by far the best of the bunch, and he initiated serious reforms of the nation's spiritual life, but the change didn't go deep enough to reverse the downward trend. Jeremiah lived at a time when people had lost their bearings and the nation was slowly disintegrating.

His ministry

Jeremiah was called to a tough task and one that lasted several decades. The message he was called to deliver as Yahweh's spokesman was both stark and clear: judgment is around the corner and cannot be avoided; spiritual adultery has consequences and, because they have broken God's covenant, Jerusalem and the temple will be destroyed and the 'chosen people' carried into exile for seventy long years of captivity.

Reading through the book of Jeremiah, we discover that he faced some formidable challenges:

- His family rejected him and some plotted to kill him.
- God expressly told him not to marry and raise children (Jeremiah 16:2).
- He was constantly accused of being a traitor to his nation.
- He was beaten and publicly abused.
- He was imprisoned and banned from any public speaking.
- He was put in the stocks and his sermons were torn up and destroyed.
- He was thrown into a well and had to be rescued by a foreigner.
- He spent time in hiding, in fear for his life.
- At the end of his life he was kidnapped, taken to Egypt and (probably) murdered.

It is apparent that Jeremiah struggled at times against this relentless opposition. In one poignant passage, he cries out to God in desperation:

> Whenever I speak, I cry out
>   proclaiming violence and destruction.
> So the word of the LORD has brought me
>   insult and reproach all day long.
> But if I say, 'I will not mention his word
>   or speak any more in his name,'

his word is in my heart like a fire,
    a fire shut up in my bones.
I am weary of holding it in;
    indeed, I cannot.
(Jeremiah 20:8–9)

Jeremiah's legacy of a lifetime of consistent, courageous service is a fitting example of what 'long obedience in the same direction' looks like.[6]

He lived to see his nation invaded by the Babylonian army and thousands of its brightest and best citizens exiled as prisoners of war. Then, a few years later, Jerusalem was destroyed and the temple burned to the ground.[7] Jeremiah had both foreseen and foretold these shattering events – with pain, not pleasure. As one writer aptly described him, Jeremiah was the prophet who wouldn't quit.[8]

His call

It's against this background that we can best understand Jeremiah's struggle in coming to terms with God's call. His was no quick-fix ministry, hurtling from nought to success in sixty seconds.

His personal account of that call takes up the opening chapter of his book. Three things stand out.

1. God's initiative

The word of the LORD came to me, saying,

'Before I formed you in the womb I knew you,
    before you were born I set you apart;
    I appointed you as a prophet to the nations.'
(Jeremiah 1:4–5)

God makes the first move, not Jeremiah. And the call was a long time in preparation – even before his parents conceived him, Yahweh had a purpose in store. The call was clear, specific and unmistakable.

2. Jeremiah's inadequacy

Yet that call is not met with an enthusiastic response, as Jeremiah feels he is too young and inexperienced:

> But I said, 'Hold it, Master GOD! Look at me.
>   I don't know anything. I'm only a boy!'
> (Jeremiah 1:6, MSG)

It is likely that Jeremiah was in his teens when this call came. He wasn't making excuses or trying to avoid a difficult task. In spite of coming from a priestly and prophetic family, he simply felt too young for the job that he was being asked to undertake. But it was more than youthful inexperience that overwhelmed him. Jeremiah felt totally inadequate for the task. He was well aware that God's message would be poorly received, and he felt untrained and out of his depth to handle such a heavy responsibility. He knew enough history to be aware of how other prophets had suffered for bringing God's Word, and he was not rushing to join the list of martyrs. Jeremiah felt utterly alone, afraid and unwilling when the call came.

3. God's response

Yahweh doesn't deny Jeremiah's youth, but he instructs him to ignore it. In words reminiscent of a formal service of ordination, God gives four statements of command and reassurance.

> 'You must go to everyone I send you to.' (Jeremiah 1:7)

'I have put my words in your mouth.' (Jeremiah 1:9)
'I am with you.' (Jeremiah 1:8)
'[I] will rescue you.' (Jeremiah 1:8)

The issues surrounding Jeremiah's sense of inadequacy are dealt a deathblow; the authority, ability, skill and security problems are God's business, and they are all taken care of.

It has been pointed out that Jeremiah's name bears a close relationship to his call. The exact meaning in Hebrew is not clear – it can be translated 'The Lord exalts' or 'The Lord hurls' – but either way the Lord (Yahweh, the personal name of God) lies at the heart of his name. Jeremiah was Yahweh's man.

He experienced the physical sensation of God touching his mouth and uttering the words of commission:

Then the LORD reached out his hand and touched my mouth and said to me, 'I have put my words in your mouth. See, today I appoint you over nations and kingdoms to uproot and tear down, to destroy and overthrow, to build and to plant.' (Jeremiah 1:9–10)

Perhaps this gives some clues to the meaning of his name: he has been raised up by the Lord (exalted) only to be thrown (hurled) into a ministry that will have both negative and positive outcomes, as some things will be torn down and new things will come into being.

The account of Jeremiah's call concludes with two visions directly linked to his ministry and some words of strength and assurance that he must have replayed over and over in his mind as the years unfolded. For example, see Jeremiah 1:17–19. The imagery of a fortified city, an iron pillar and a bronze wall convey the sense of immovability. How often in his darkest moments Jeremiah must have turned to the promise of the Lord: ' "They will fight against you but will not overcome you, for I am with you and will rescue you," declares the LORD.'

Learning from the story

If you have ever been asked to do a job bigger than you imagined, you'll know the kinds of questions that tumble around your head:

- Am I up to it?
- Surely there are others who can do this better?
- How will I cope?
- What will happen when everyone finds out I'm useless?
- When I fail, will I ever live it down?

I was once nominated for an elected post. Part of me was flattered that some people had believed in me enough to put my name forward. But at the same time, these very questions gnawed at me. I felt overawed by the size of the task (which looking back was no big deal – but at the time it was!). An honest chat with a close friend was a great help. He listened patiently as I ran through the checklist of my insecurities. I gave him all the reasons why I couldn't and shouldn't let my name stand. I presented my case well and finished with a flourish: 'Besides, I can think of several people who could do the job far better than me!'

My friend paused for several seconds before delivering the killer blow. 'You're right – there are people who could do a better job. But you are still the right person for the job, because God wants to teach you things through it.'

It was one of those 'game, set and match' moments. There was nothing left to be said, because deep down I sensed that

God was calling me to take on a task that was made for me – not because I was the best person, but the right person. And it is an experience that I have faced several times since that memorable moment.

Perhaps you can identify with this, and maybe it strikes a chord with something you are facing right now.

Three lessons stand out from Jeremiah's postcard from the edge.

1. When God calls someone, he always provides the tools for the job

Jeremiah was no stranger to feelings of inadequacy – in fact, it was a recurring struggle in his life. These feelings didn't vanish when God called him in chapter 1; as for all of us, his insecurities bubbled up to the surface in times of stress. What he had to discover was that God would provide what was needed to overcome these feelings of inadequacy. The lesson for us is that we need to live with the fact that, for whatever reason, we will sometimes feel that the job is too big and our abilities too small. On the positive side, it is always better to feel that way than to be brimful of misplaced pride and overconfidence.

2. God measures success differently

Was Jeremiah successful? The answer depends on how you view success. If it is measured by ratings in the opinion polls, material benefits and a comfortable life, then Jeremiah failed totally. But if you believe that the smile from heaven matters more and that there is a life to come where rewards and honours will eclipse the best that this world can offer, then Jeremiah has yet to have his day. We should take heart from his example.

3. God prizes faithfulness

Hebrews 11 lists some of the great heroes and heroines of faith, and stands as a reminder that God misses nothing and prizes greatly the faithfulness of those called to serve him. Their lives stand as a testament and encouragement to us to run well the race set out for us (see Hebrews 12:1–3). Jeremiah is in that hall of fame, described well by Eugene Peterson as 'determinedly faithful, magnificently courageous, heartlessly rejected – a towering life terrifically lived'.[9]

So what?

- Is a sense of inadequacy a vice or a virtue?
- What are some of the most common areas of insecurity surrounding our capability to undertake a task?
- How can you be sure that God is calling you to do something?
- Was Jeremiah successful?
- What encouragement would you offer Jo, whose story began this chapter?
- What can you most identify with from Jeremiah's postcard?
- Do you know someone overwhelmed with feelings of inadequacy? What can you do to encourage them?

Frodo's story

'I am not made for perilous quests,' cried Frodo. 'I wish I had never seen the Ring! Why did it come to me? Why was I chosen?'

'Such questions cannot be answered,' said Gandalf. 'You may be sure that it was not for any merit that others do not possess; not for power or wisdom, at any rate. But you have been chosen and you must therefore use such strength and heart and wits as you have.'[10]

Jeremiah sits uncomfortably in a noisy culture that clamours for easy solutions, instant success and celebrity. He offers a more rugged, persistent description of a life of faith. His faith caused him to embrace his inadequacies, even celebrate them, in order to give himself completely to the greater purpose of God.

In doing so, Jeremiah reveals a richer seam of faith that lies beneath the surface.

For it is only in suffering, as all the New Testament writers attest to, that deep faith is forged. If we insist on bypassing suffering to resort to a gospel of pleasant optimism, then all we will have is an attenuated faith: happy songs for happy people, for an oh-so-happy God. We will never discover the depths of a faith hammered out on the anvil of pain. Vast tracts of our emotional terrain will be left unexplored.[11]

5. JOHN THE BAPTIST AND DOUBT

Setting the scene

I was about seven years old the first time I was conned.

On the long walk home from school one sunny afternoon, as I passed by some woods, an older boy showed me a large bush that was big enough to crawl inside. We wriggled our way through to the centre, where it was big enough to sit side by side. As we sat there, he told me that as well as being big enough to hide in, the bush had special magical powers. If you wished hard enough and long enough, the bush would make your wishes come true. (Bear in mind that when you're seven, stuff like that sounds plausible.)

However, there were two conditions attached to this arrangement. First, you had to give the one providing this information (in my case, the older boy sitting with me in the bush) a suitable sum of money in consideration. Secondly, the bush worked on a twenty-four-hour cycle, so whatever you wished for today couldn't be collected until tomorrow.

My tiny mind was blown by the whole idea. Apparently there was no limit to the length of the wish-list, but my new-found friend suggested that I go easy to start with and limit myself to a few items the first time around. I emptied my pockets of the few coins I had and began to compile my wish-list. I can't remember how long I sat there, but I do recall that the modest list included a brand new bike plus a few other toys that I had my eye on.

With my wish-list made, all I had to do was wait for an agonizingly slow day to pass until the school bell rang at 3.20 the next afternoon.

I felt like I broke several running records racing to the scene of my reward. The boy had told me that this was a secret that must not be shared, and I had kept my solemn promise to tell no-one, although it had been so hard to keep that part of the deal as the build-up of excitement through the day had made me fit to burst.

When I reached the bush, there was not a soul in sight, so I dived in and crawled into its leafy centre, brimful of confidence that my prizes would be waiting.

Were they heck.

I searched in vain for several minutes, eventually trudging home with empty hands and a very heavy heart.

Seven years old, cheated, made to feel stupid, too embarrassed to tell anyone and feeling very alone. And, yes, a bit wiser about the way the world works.

Not everyone can be trusted. Not everyone tells the truth. Some people tell lies and take things from you. People you believe in can let you down. A little piece of my trust fell to the ground and died that day.

On the plus side, I learned some important life lessons from what is sometimes called the school of hard knocks. But on the downside, my confidence and ability to trust were dented.

And since that incident, over fifty years ago, a great many more dents have been added.

Most of us have been let down by others and, if we are honest, most of us have let others down too. I have met people who have faced the worst kinds of betrayal, and listening to their stories has made me wonder how they could trust anyone again.

But for followers of Jesus Christ, words such as *faith*, *trust*, *confidence* and *obedience* are the common language of discipleship. Can these qualities live alongside words like *doubt*, *questions* and *insecurity*?

In this chapter, we are looking at an incident in the life of a man described by Jesus as 'a lamp that burned and gave light' (John 5:35) as he prepared the way for the coming Messiah. John was last in the great line of Old Testament prophets, a man of great moral strength and character. But he was also someone who struggled with doubt.

He knew what it was to have his confidence dented.

Listening to the story – Luke 7:18–35

John the Baptist had of course earned his nickname through baptizing people.[1] And that came about because of God's remarkable call on his life. To put it simply, John was called to prepare the way of the Lord and then get out of the way of the Lord. His public career was short – probably only a few months. His public preaching had a big impact, and his call for people to sort their lives out with God led many to confess their sins and be baptized in the River Jordan. But John consistently pointed out that he was not the headline act; someone bigger and better was expected – the long-awaited Messiah.

At what point John discovered that his cousin, Jesus of Nazareth, was that Messiah we don't know, but the moment he first pointed him out to others remains memorable: 'Look, the Lamb of God, who takes away the sin of the world!' (John 1:29).

But we pick up the story when life had changed for John and the crowds were no longer flocking to hear his dynamic preaching. He had openly challenged Herod Antipas' behaviour for marrying his sister-in-law, Herodias, and the powerful monarch had had him thrown into jail.[2] Prophets who question the status quo are rarely tolerated by those they challenge.

John was a man of the desert who lived in wide-open spaces. Now he was confined to a cell in Herod's palace, the monotony broken only by occasional audiences with the curious king (Mark 6:17–20) and perhaps abbreviated visits from his friends. The cramped isolation played havoc with his mind. A preacher of a previous generation captured John's dilemma well:

> He pined with the hunger of a wild thing for liberty – to move without the clanking fetters; to drink the fresh water of the Jordan; to breathe the morning air; to look on the expanse of nature. Is it hard to understand how his deprivations reacted on his mental and spiritual organisations, or that his nervous system lost that elasticity of tone, or that the depression of his physical life cast a shadow on his soul?[3]

The language is of another era, but it describes John's isolation and its impact. He began to have doubts, and news from the outside world did little to ease his troubled mind.

What was Jesus up to? Why were things not turning out the way John had spoken about so passionately? 'The axe has been laid to the root of the trees, and every tree that does not produce good fruit will be cut down and thrown into the fire,'

John had preached to the crowds. 'But after me comes one who is more powerful than I, whose sandals I am not worthy to carry. He will baptise you with the Holy Spirit and fire. His winnowing fork is in his hand, and he will clear his threshing-floor, gathering his wheat into the barn and burning up the chaff with unquenchable fire' (Matthew 3:10–12).

But the report from John's disciples simply didn't square with this. There was no axe, no fire and no clearing of the threshing-floor. Jesus wasn't acting in the way that John had said he would.

Whatever John had anticipated, it wasn't happening. Gnawing at his restless mind was a question that tortured him during the long, lonely hours hunched in a dark prison cell: 'Have I made a terrible mistake?'

We can't begin to imagine the mental torture that John experienced as he wrestled with this question. He had been called to prepare the way for someone and something of cosmic significance. What if he had got it wrong? What if the real Messiah was someone else, someone now confined to obscurity because John got it wrong? Had he derailed God's plan? Was he responsible for the biggest mistake ever? Would he go down in history not as a forerunner but as a failure? Was his whole ministry, and now his imprisonment, for nothing?

John waited with these gnawing doubts as he sent two of his trusted friends to Jesus to put the anxious question: 'Are you the one who is to come, or should we expect someone else?' (Luke 7:19).

The way that Jesus dealt with his doubting cousin reveals something of God's compassion to those of us who wrestle with doubts.

Perhaps the first thing to notice is what *doesn't* happen. Jesus doesn't issue a stinging rebuke or caustic comment. There is no trace of 'How could you be so pathetic?' On the contrary, Jesus goes out of his way to commend the fortitude and courage of his cousin. He sends the friends back with a message filled with good news – and adds a personal note of encouragement. A message of hope for those moments of doubt: 'Blessed is anyone who does not stumble on account of me' (Luke 7:23).

Learning from the story

Looking at how Jesus replied to John's burning question offers us some insights on how to deal with doubt. Jesus' reply to John can be viewed at three levels.

1. *He points to what God is doing*

Jesus tells John's friends to go back to the prison with eye-witness accounts of what is happening. When you are in jail, time is heavy on your hands. Hearing news of blind people seeing for the first time, lame people walking and those suffering from leprosy being healed and restored to community life brings a different perspective! Then there are those who have died being miraculously restored to life, and those at the bottom of the pile receiving the good news of God's blessing (Luke 7:22). Here were stories of hope to revive John's spirit and renew his courage.

Too often we confine our understanding of what God is doing to the limitations of our own four walls. Like John in his lonely cell, we remain trapped by our own limited perspective. Lifting our heads and opening our eyes to the wider picture helps us to grasp the greater reality.

This was reinforced for me recently in preparing to write this book. I came across Dan Meyer's book, *Witness Essentials*,[4] in which he lists some encouraging statistics about the growth of the church around the world. Here's a taster:

- In 1900, Korea had no Protestant church. Today [2012], there are over 7,000 churches in just the city of Seoul, South Korea. Almost 30% of the population claim Christian allegiance.
- At the end of the nineteenth century, the southern portion of Africa was only 3% Christian. Today, 63% of the population is Christian, while membership in the churches in Africa is increasing by 34,000 people per day.
- In India, 14 million of the 140 million members of the Dalit 'untouchable' caste have become Christians in recent years.
- More people in the Islamic world have come to Christ in the last twenty-five years than in the entire history of Christian missions.
- In Islamic Indonesia, the percentage of Christians is now so high (around 15%) that the Muslim government will no longer print statistics.
- In China, it is estimated that there are now more self-avowed disciples of Jesus than there are members of the Communist Party. Even the most conservative estimates suggest that China will soon have more Christians than any country.
- Across the planet, followers of Jesus are increasing by more than 80,000 per day.
- It is estimated that across the globe, 510 new churches form every day.

Meyer concludes: 'The irony is that, except for the Middle East (where Christianity was born) and Europe and America (to whose civilization it gave birth), Christianity is expanding everywhere today.'

2. *He reminds him of what God has said*
The message that Jesus sent to John had an element of code about it. John knew the book of the prophet Isaiah well; it gave

him the foundation for his ministry as the trailblazer of the Messiah.[5] He had pored over the message of this prophet and soaked himself in the words of the book. When challenged by the religious authorities, John claimed he was the voice in the desert that the prophet had foreseen and foretold. In the Ancient Near East, it was customary for representatives to be sent ahead to prepare the way for the coming monarch. Isaiah used that image to describe someone who would be the forerunner for the Messiah. John attributes that role to himself (see John 1:23).

So the full impact of Jesus' message would not have been lost on John as he weighed the reply relayed by his friends. He would recall the words spoken by the Messiah in Isaiah's vision of the future:

> The Spirit of GOD, the Master, is on me
>> because GOD anointed me.
> He sent me to preach good news to the poor,
>> heal the heartbroken,
> Announce freedom to all captives,
>> pardon all prisoners.
> GOD sent me to announce the year of his grace –
>> a celebration of God's destruction of our enemies –
>> and to comfort all who mourn,
> To care for the needs of all who mourn in Zion,
>> give them bouquets of roses instead of ashes,
> Messages of joy instead of news of doom,
>> a praising heart instead of a languid spirit.
> Rename them 'Oaks of Righteousness'
>> planted by GOD to display his glory.
> (Isaiah 61:1–3, MSG)[6]

John's friends brought news of healing, deliverance and joy for those who were often last in the queue. In other words,

Jesus was fulfilling what Isaiah has seen and declared hundreds of years before. John hadn't made a mistake in wrongly identifying Jesus; his mistake was in not fully understanding what Jesus had come to accomplish.

John's message was heavy on repentance and the need for people to change their behaviour.[7] The act of being baptized in water served as a symbol of washing away those things that stained, and so the crowds who responded to John's preaching came acknowledging their need of a fresh start (Matthew 3:6). From what we read of his sermons, John stressed that a day of reckoning was coming, and this added the note of urgency to his preaching. People needed to be repentant and ready, because God was on the move! Tucked in the middle of the passage from Isaiah 61 was a mention of 'the day of vengeance of our God' (v. 2), but John needed reminding that this was not the whole message. There was good news for the poor, freedom for captives, beauty for ashes and joy for broken hearts.

The message Jesus sent via John's friends reminded him of *all* that God had said through Isaiah's prophecy, not just part of it.

John hadn't got the message wrong, but his understanding of its timing was out. As the Apostles' Creed affirms, Jesus will return 'to judge the living and the dead', and the day of reckoning prophesied by Isaiah and preached by John will be fulfilled.

3. He promises God's blessing for those who doubt, yet trust

The final part of the message that Jesus sent back to John has been called 'The Ninth Beatitude'.[8] It is words of blessing for a man who needed encouragement. Translated literally, the message Jesus sent reads, 'Blessed is whoever is not offended in me.'

Jesus hadn't been acting in the way that John had hoped, and so was causing him to trip up or stumble. The blessing, according to Jesus, comes to those who trust without fully understanding why things happen the way they sometimes do.

We can't always see the whole picture or make sense of circumstances that seem uncontrolled. Like John in his lonely prison cell, we can feel isolated and afraid. At such moments, we have a clear choice. We can either exercise trust or give way to doubt. The first is the way of faith, and the other the route of unbelief.

The best definition of faith that I have come across is contained in just two words: believing God. Not believing *in* God (according to James, even demons can do that – see James 2:19), but actually *believing* God. This calls us to trust at those times when the way ahead is far from clear.

Jesus' promise to John was that there is a special blessing for those who exercise that kind of trust in moments of darkness.

Luke then tells us that as John's friends set off, Jesus turned to the surrounding crowd and issued a stunning public endorsement: 'I tell you, among those born of women there is no one greater than John; yet the one who is least in the kingdom of God is greater than he' (Luke 7:28).

The first part is a clear assessment of Jesus' estimation of his cousin, but the second part of the sentence appears confusing. It is best understood when we consider that with John's ministry, an old order was ending and a new one beginning. In the long line of prophets, John takes the place of honour, according to Jesus. But now, with the arrival of the King and the coming of the kingdom, a new day is dawning. Here's how one writer expressed it:

John marked a dividing line in history. Since John's proclamation had been made Jesus had come; eternity had invaded time; heaven had invaded earth; God had arrived in Jesus; and therefore life could never be the same again. We date all time as before Christ and after Christ – BC and AD. Jesus is the dividing line. And, therefore, all who come after him and who receive him are of necessity granted a greater blessing than all who went before. The entry of Jesus into the world divided all time into two; and the entry of Jesus into our lives divided all life in two.[9]

But Jesus' endorsement of John sends an important signal to us. John's doubt and questions hadn't lessened his Lord's love for him. John was no reed swayed by the wind, nor a self-indulgent seeker after celebrity, according to Jesus. This was affirmation of the highest order, which makes me wonder if – in the life to come – what we view now as our darkest moments may prove to have been our finest hours.

Taking the three-level response of Jesus to John's doubt, we pick up some helpful pointers. When doubts strike:

- Look at the bigger picture to see what God is doing, not just the immediate circumstances.
- Remember what God has promised.
- Expect the blessing that comes for those who trust when it's dark.

I was once challenged by a close friend as I weighed an important decision. 'You want God to map it all out, don't you? To show how it will all work out?' My guard was down and I admitted that he'd summed up my feelings well. That was when the killer punch landed.

'Where's the faith in that?' my friend asked.

So what?

- What triggers your doubts?
- Are there aspects of John's dilemma with which you identify? What are they?
- John emphasized the judgment of God, yet seemed to forget the promise of his mercy and love. Do you think we sometimes make the opposite mistake? How can we find balance?
- What have you found most helpful in times of doubt?
- It's been said that if you feed your faith, you starve your doubts to death. Is this true? If so, how do we feed our faith?
- How can we focus on the big picture of what God is doing in a given situation?

Albert's story

One of the most iconic images of the twentieth century is the face of Albert Einstein, the Nobel Prize winner, who looked like the stereotypical mad professor. With a face like that, you would be recognized anywhere.

One day, travelling on a suburban train in Princeton, a ticket collector spotted the professor searching anxiously through his pockets, trying to locate his ticket. The official put him at his ease. 'Sir, please don't worry. I recognize you and you're a regular traveller. I am sure you have a ticket – enjoy your day.'

Some time later, the collector passed back through the carriage to find Einstein on his knees, searching under the seat for the lost ticket. The man helped him to his feet, insisting, 'Please sir, don't trouble yourself. I know who you are!' To which the professor replied, 'Young man, I know you know who I am. I know who I am. But what I don't know is where I'm meant to be going!'

It's encouraging to know that you might be able to articulate the theory of relativity and still not be able to remember where you are going.

But followers of Jesus know where they are going:

> Do not let your hearts be troubled. You believe in God; believe also in me. My Father's house has many rooms; if that were not so, would I have told you that I am going there to prepare a place for you? And if I go and prepare a place for you, I will come back and take you to be with me that you also may be where I am. You know the way to the place where I am going. (John 14:1–4)

At times when doubts make us question what is happening, it's important to hold on to the big picture and to remember what God's Word tells us about who we are, whose we are and where, ultimately, we are going.

It is not recorded that Jesus ever said, 'Believe my arguments', but he did say, on more than one occasion, 'Believe me.'

And part of the challenge of following Jesus is the call to believe and leave the explanations for later.

6. JOHN MARK AND FAILURE

Setting the scene

I was asked to review a book some years ago, and this is part of what I wrote:

> It's sad, but true, that the Christian Army often shoots its wounded. MacDonald – a man whose own world has been broken, and is gradually being rebuilt – writes with gut-wrenching honesty. He explores the reasons why Christians fall and then examines the ways in which God can rebuild what is broken. Although challenging, it is a book that speaks from the heart to the heart. When I started to read, I could hardly put it down because of its deep insights . . . if you're a 'broken world' person, or you care for those who are, this book is gold dust.[1]

The author, Gordon MacDonald, wrote the book *Rebuilding Your Broken World*[2] in the aftermath of his personal failure as a husband, father and pastor. He admits to an adulterous relationship and, in his words, 'I betrayed the covenants of my marriage. There was a moment when I brought deep sorrow to my wife, to my children, and to friends and others who had trusted me for years.'[3]

He skilfully avoids any sensationalizing of his sin and he offers no excuses about the circumstances that led to his wrongdoing. Instead, the book is an exploration of how God puts our broken lives together again through his restoring, healing grace. In the nursery rhyme, Humpty Dumpty had no chance of being put back together. But the gospel is no nursery rhyme, and MacDonald explains his own insider journey of restoration through the glue of grace.

Since all this happened in the 1980s, I have met Gordon MacDonald. Of all the people I have ever met, he is one of those who has impressed me most. There is a godly humility that comes with a limp, a little like Jacob's (see Genesis 32:31).

But very few Christian leaders survive moral failure, and those who try to come back into ministry find that journey very hard. As various people have observed, integrity is like virginity – once it's gone, it's gone.

Failure comes in a variety of colours and shades. For MacDonald, it was a sexual relationship outside of his marriage commitment, which by the Bible's standards is sin. And for a preacher and pastor, it is a more public sin than for most.

But sometimes failure is simply failure. A business goes to the wall; we are fired from our job; we are told we are no longer needed in a team or we didn't make the shortlist for interview.

Most of us find relationship failures the hardest to live with – a marriage that ends in divorce, children who challenge our parenting abilities or family members who make unpleasant accusations.

Whatever the colour or shade, failure always leaves an ugly stain.

Listening to the story

Naked runaway – Mark 14:51–52

John Mark became involved in the Christian faith through the influence of his family. His mother, Mary, owned a house in Jerusalem that became a base for the Christian community. (See Acts 12:12, where the church gathered to pray on hearing of Peter's arrest.)

John Mark's father is not mentioned, which suggests either that he had died or that he did not share his wife's faith. It could even be that Mary's house was the location that Jesus chose for the Last Supper, which may explain a curious comment in the Gospel that John Mark wrote:

> A young man, wearing nothing but a linen garment, was
> following Jesus. When they seized him, he fled naked,
> leaving his garment behind.
> (Mark 14:51–52)

It may be that this was none other than John Mark himself, adding himself anonymously into his Gospel record. Perhaps disturbed by Jesus and the disciples' late meal and maybe with a sense of foreboding, the young man rose from his bed wrapped in nothing but a sheet, and followed the group to the Garden of Gethsemane. It would appear that Jesus' arrest prompted a scuffle, during which someone seized the young observer, who wriggled free of their grasp and ran naked into the night.

Part of the team – Acts 12:25 – 13:12

John Mark appears again in the unfolding story of Jesus, when Barnabas and Saul recruit him as an assistant to their ministry team – a move which is not that surprising, as we are told that he is related to Barnabas.[4] He joins their work with the emerging church in Antioch, and when the bold decision is taken to release Barnabas and Saul to wider ministry, John Mark goes along as a travelling companion.[5] This type of apprenticeship in ministry is often very effective, as someone young and inexperienced is able to shadow others and learn on the job. Their first port of call was the island of Cyprus (Barnabas' home,[6] so possibly a place where John Mark had other relatives).

The missionary team travelled across the island and ended up at the western port of Paphos, where the Roman governor had his palace and military and administrative base. News had reached him about the preaching of Barnabas and Saul, and Luke (who wrote the book of Acts) records that the governor, Sergius Paulus, asked to see them in order to find out more about their message.

In an astonishing encounter with a Jewish sorcerer who tried to put the governor off from listening to the message about Jesus Christ, Saul confronts the man and he is temporarily struck blind. Luke details that the governor was led to faith in Christ through witnessing this power encounter.

What went wrong? – Acts 13:13

This meeting at the governor's palace was a landmark event for several reasons. First, it is the earliest record of a senior Roman official being converted. Secondly, it marks the emergence of Paul in his apostolic ministry; from now on the narrative records Paul and Barnabas instead of Barnabas and Saul.[7] Thirdly, John Mark decided to leave the team and return to Jerusalem.

What went wrong for John Mark? What made him leave the team, especially after witnessing the remarkable conversion of a powerful man? We can only speculate as to what motivated the decision to sail home. Some suggest that it was a simple case of homesickness. Perhaps John Mark was especially close to his mother, Mary, and this represented the longest time they had been apart. Not everyone can cope with the demands of travel and adapting to strange surroundings. Others have suggested that he had been ill and that the travel schedule was not helping his recovery, so he decided to go home to convalesce. In my view, what is more likely is that John Mark found the going too tough, and the encounter with the Jewish sorcerer, Elymas, was simply a bridge too far. John Mark was astute enough to realize that this sort of thing was likely to happen again – only next time, it might lead to a violent attack on the messengers themselves. Putting it bluntly, he lost his nerve.

Fallout between friends – Acts 15:36–41

Several months had passed after Paul and Barnabas had returned to Antioch after what we know as the first missionary journey.[8] Paul suggested a return trip to all the congregations that they had established. Barnabas agreed and suggested that John Mark join them. Paul's response was emphatic: in his view, John Mark had deserted them and was not worthy of a second chance. Luke records that the two friends had a sharp disagreement,[9] which led to them going their separate ways. Paul recruited Silas as his new team member, and they set off on the planned trip. Barnabas (ever the encourager) took John Mark under his wing and they returned to Cyprus, the place where it had all fallen apart. We have no record of Paul and Barnabas working together again.[10]

A new beginning – 2 Timothy 4:9–13

We are not entirely sure how it happened, but we do know that John Mark was reconciled to Paul – and more than that, he became a valued member of Paul's team.

Piecing the evidence together, it seems that Barnabas' ministry of encouragement paid off and John Mark became linked to Peter, the disciple. The two of them worked together in Rome, where Peter drew together his eyewitness account of the ministry of Jesus and invited John Mark to write it all down.

The friendship and support of these two men, Barnabas and Peter, paid off, and somewhere along the line, the links with Paul were restored. When Paul writes his letter to the church at Colossae, Mark is commended in warm terms (Colossians 4:10). In writing his personal letter to Philemon, Paul refers to Mark as one of his 'fellow workers' (Philemon 24). But the most special reference of all comes in the last recorded letter that we have from Paul's pen. His sense of loneliness comes through as he concludes his second letter to Timothy. He feels deserted by some and opposed by others, but he sends this vital message: 'Get Mark and bring him with you, because he is helpful to me in my ministry' (2 Timothy 4:11).

John Mark made it back from failure, and a story that could have ended in personal brokenness and disaster was turned around by the grace of God. Every time we pick up Mark's Gospel and read it, we are reminded that failure needn't end in failure.

Learning from the story

If you have experienced failure, you will know it is not easy to rid yourself of the aftertaste. It can linger for a long time.

Unless it is dealt with effectively, it leaves lasting damage. Looking at John Mark's five recovery steps shows us how failure can be used positively and as an opportunity for growth.

1. *He was willing to face his failure*
He must have accepted what had happened, even if he couldn't fully understand or explain why he had chosen to leave Cyprus and go home early. It can take time for the dust to settle, especially when our emotions are extra sensitive. John Mark may not have been able to work out all that was going on until he had some distance from the incident. He may never have got to the bottom of all that was happening at that difficult time in his life. But when he came to the point of accepting his failure, he was ready to learn lessons that would help in future.

We often need help at this stage of the journey. People we trust who can stand apart from what has gone on are often ideally placed to help. I have friends who have received support through the fellowship of Alcoholics Anonymous, and they remind me that each session begins with a personal acknowledgment along the lines of: 'My name is Rob and I am an alcoholic.'

You may not have touched a drop for twenty years, but it's an important acknowledgment of what has happened and the path that your life has taken.

2. *He was willing to accept help*
Cousin Barnabas offered to take John Mark on his journey to Cyprus, which in itself was a generous gesture after the split with Paul. But it would have been easy for John Mark to take offence at Paul's rejection and refuse the opportunity of future ministry. Equally, when Peter befriended him and sought his assistance in writing his eyewitness account of Jesus, John Mark could have pleaded special circumstances and

opted out. Life on the sidelines must have looked tempting, but he accepted the help that was offered by people who genuinely cared for his welfare. As a result, John Mark found his way back on to the pitch.

Accepting help requires a degree of humility on our part, and that can be especially hard if we have a strongly self-sufficient character. You may enjoy a reputation for sorting everyone else's problems out, and it will take grace to admit that, this time around, you need others to help you.

3. He was prepared to start again

Like getting behind the wheel of a car after a serious accident, John Mark knew he had to face the challenge of ministry once again. Revisiting Cyprus probably raised some awkward questions as well as provoking memories. His decision to take up the reins of responsibility was born of courage and shows the character of the man.

The road from failure to recovery may mean returning to well-known places and meeting familiar faces. But there is no alternative if we want to start over. This is where the power of relationship proves its worth. Barnabas was at John Mark's shoulder throughout the journey, and his very presence was the kind of vote of confidence that could answer potential critics. We all need friends like that when we decide to start again.

4. He was ready to learn from past mistakes

Paul's objection to Barnabas' suggestion to take John Mark with them a second time was that the latter had proved himself to be useless. John Mark's decision to return home may have been triggered by any number of things, as has already been discussed: fear, homesickness, struggles with his health or something else. But the fact that he was willing to try again strongly suggests he had learned lessons from his past experience that stood him in good stead for the future.

When Paul longs for his company and describes him as 'helpful to me in my ministry' (2 Timothy 4:11), it is poignant testimony to John Mark's progress. Paul had changed his opinion based on John Mark's progress in learning from and profiting by his past mistakes.

5. He was open to receive forgiveness

When forgiveness is mentioned in a Christian context, we automatically think of it in relation to God. The entry point into the Christian family is our willingness to acknowledge our need of God's forgiveness, which is made available through the atoning death of Jesus Christ on the cross. Our need to have the slate wiped clean, and the remarkable offer of forgiveness being possible through the completed work of Jesus, lies at the very heart of our faith (see John 3:14–17; Colossians 2:13–15; 1 John 1:8–9).

But forgiveness is a vast river that overflows its banks to bring release to others. The arms of the cross of Christ stretch horizontally as well as vertically. When an individual is reconciled to God, it follows that broken relationships with others may also be healed. In the words of the Lord's Prayer, 'Forgive us our sins, for we also forgive everyone who sins against us. And lead us not into temptation' (Luke 11:4).

In John Mark's case, he needed to receive forgiveness as well as to extend it to those (which might include Paul) who he felt had treated him unfairly. Most of all – and this was possibly the hardest task – he would need to forgive himself. Forgiveness is a liberating experience, and its source is grace from God himself: Father, Son and Holy Spirit (2 Corinthians 13:14).

John Mark made the journey back from failure and became useful in the work of God's kingdom. He refused to be defined by his failure to stick it out with Barnabas and Saul on their earlier missionary trip. By his positive responses outlined above, he made his difficult experience a platform from which to climb to higher things. He shows that failure needn't be the last word, but can be the start of a whole new chapter.

So what?

- Think of an experience of failure in your life. What have you learned from it?
- This comment was made just above about John Mark: 'He made his difficult experience a platform from which to climb to higher things. He shows that failure needn't be the last word, but can be the start of a whole new chapter.' How do you respond to this claim?
- Look at the five steps that outline John Mark's positive response. Which one do you think was the hardest? Which would you struggle with most?
- Is there such a thing as failure from which we can never recover?
- What can we say to someone who finds it impossible to forgive and move on?
- What can you take from John Mark's experience to help in your own growth?

My story

Some years ago, I was called to be the senior pastor of an international church in Europe. The circumstances surrounding the call were unusual (in some senses, dramatic), and it led to big changes for our whole family. There were lots of adjustments we needed to make and, by God's grace, we managed them reasonably well. We enjoyed the challenge and opportunities of living in another country and adapting to a different culture. The church was made up of around sixty nationalities and a heady mix of Christian traditions, all of which made pastoring constantly interesting, sometimes frustrating, often confusing – but never boring!

After a few years, the church hit a crisis. In part it was financial, but that was really the tip of an iceberg. After a painful few months, my wife Ruth and I concluded that I had no alternative than to resign. This decision came after some deep heart-searching and prayer on our part, through which we realized that I didn't have the confidence and support of the church members.

Our resignation was not well received. Not everyone understood what lay behind it, and some (understandably) felt angry at what they saw as our betrayal. We offered to work our notice period and help sort some underlying issues, but this was turned down. I was summoned to a meeting on a Thursday and told to preach on Sunday, immediately after which it would be publicly announced that I was no longer the pastor. I agreed to preach, but persuaded them to delay saying anything publicly until after the weekend.

It was a tough Sunday.

At the end of the two morning services, I left the building and walked into an uncertain future.

Circumstances meant that we had to continue living in our rented accommodation for another eight months before we returned to the UK. I was fifty-six years of age, with no job to go to and nowhere to live.

God was wonderfully close and our relationship as a couple deepened through the crisis. Friends stood by us and showed love and practical care in ways beyond our comprehension.

But as the months passed, my personal struggles grew more intense. There were questions that haunted my daytime hours and kept me awake most nights. They boiled down to a single, stark fact.

I was a failed leader.

The conclusion that I no longer had the confidence of this Christian community went deep.

Leadership is defined by influence. As I constantly tell my students, if you want to know if you're a leader, then look over your shoulder. If no-one is following, then you're not leading but just having a walk.

Well, I was looking over my shoulder, and there was no-one to be seen for miles.

Like John Mark, I have found that time has given perspective to my circumstances. By God's grace I am in a different place. As I write these words, there are scars, but no open wounds.

God used different people and various experiences to bring about this work of healing. One particular conversation stands out in my memory.

It came during the final weeks of preparing to move back to the UK. I had been offered an exciting new post, we had somewhere to live and our precarious financial situation had been miraculously dealt with. The light was shining brightly at the end of the proverbial tunnel.

But for all these encouragements, I was suffering from a battered spirit, with one constant question gnawing at my mind: 'What has all this been about?'

My despairing assessment of four years of hard work was simple. I had inherited a mess, made a mess and left a bigger mess.

One morning, Nathan Fisher rang. Nathan was a pastor and close friend who had kept in regular touch during our time overseas. We had a no-nonsense kind of friendship that had grown out of a shared journey in ministry. I knew I was safe in opening my heart to Nathan. He patiently pointed out the good things that God had in store, and the way that doors were opening not closing. He did his best to lift my head. But I wasn't listening. I was preoccupied with that nagging question: 'What has all this been about?'

Nathan cut in with an answer that brought sense to my confusion. 'If I decided to take up boxing,' he said, 'I'd never trust a coach who didn't have a broken nose. Now you've got a broken nose.'

He was absolutely right.

And in the many opportunities that come my way to encourage leaders, I can never stand to speak or sit to write without remembering that.

'My name is Ian – and I have a broken nose.'

7. PAUL AND FEAR

Setting the scene

I am scared of heights. One day, something needed to be fixed on the roof of our house, and I knew I would have to overcome this fear and sort the problem. I managed to clamber up on to the roof and carry out the small repair. But when I came to climb back on the ladder, I was overwhelmed with a feeling of panic. I was convinced that the ladder would move as soon as I put my weight on the top rung. And the longer I sat there, the more my terror increased. My wife, Ruth, came into the garden to see why I was taking so long. She spotted that I was in trouble and offered to hold the ladder to prevent it moving – but that didn't calm me. She fetched rope and secured the ladder to a drainpipe – but that didn't help much either. By now I had convinced myself that the ladder was unsafe and that the moment I swung my leg across, it would slide and send me plunging to the patio. I could even visualize the squidgy mess that would have once been me lying lifeless between the barbecue and the paddling pool. I was frozen with fear. And there I sat for some considerable time, trying everything I could think of to convince myself that my fear was irrational. But I was stuck.

My enterprising life partner, however, was not. She announced the obvious solution – she would call the fire brigade.

I experienced a 'defining moment' as I contemplated the consequences of this. We lived in a small community, on the main road that ran through the village. Our neighbours were nice but nosey, and there was no way a blue-lighted fire engine screaming up outside our house at eight o'clock in the evening would escape attention. Nor would the sight of a middle-aged man being lifted off a roof pass unnoticed. My mind began to clear as I weighed a stark choice. I could die smashed on the patio or I could die every day of embarrassment, celebrated as the man who had to be lifted off the roof of his house because he was too scared to climb down. Pointing fingers, malicious whispers and ridiculing stares. Ugh!

Male pride won the day, and I made it to the ground safe and sound.

Even typing this has caused my palms to sweat as I recall one of the scariest moments of my life. But that incident taught me three valuable life lessons. First, fear distorts your perception. Secondly, it paralyses your actions. Thirdly, if you want to get your roof fixed, pay someone to do it. For the purposes of this chapter, the third lesson is not important – but the other two are.

Fear creates an inability to think clearly. Like the warning on some car mirrors, things can appear larger than they actually are. Blind panic can also cause a paralysis of action. We become rooted to the spot – the phrase 'frozen with fear' says it all.

Christians are not immune to fear (perhaps that's why 'Fear not' is repeated many times in the Bible). And for a postcard from the edge on this topic, we turn to the Christian leader Paul.

Listening to the story – Acts 18:1–11

Paul was the player who showed up after the kick-off or, in his own words, he was 'abnormally born' (1 Corinthians 15:8) – that is, he was converted probably five years after the death and resurrection of the Lord Jesus Christ. He was a man of extraordinary gifts and abilities.

A present-day parallel has been suggested in a man who could lecture in Beijing in Chinese, quoting Confucius and Mencius, who could write closely argued theology and teach it at Oxford University, and who could defend his case in Moscow before the Academy of Sciences in fluent Russian.[1] We could be forgiven for doubting that such a talented individual could ever be dogged by fear.

But the passage from Acts 18 tells of a crisis in Paul's life during the course of a visit to the bustling seaport of Corinth, a commercial city visited by traders from across the known world. It was a multi-faith centre with temples to many gods and goddesses, the most infamous being the one dedicated to Aphrodite who, in Greek mythology, was the goddess of love, beauty and sexual pleasure (the word 'aphrodisiac' comes from her name). So-called sacred prostitution was on offer as part of the worship ritual, and it played a part in Corinth's growth in wealth and reputation. During the first century AD, Corinth was a byword for immorality. The phrase 'Corinthian woman' was slang for a prostitute, a Corinthian in a Greek play was typecast as a drunken lecher and a new word was born in Greek when 'to Corinthianize' described the process of dragging an individual's personal standards down to the level of the gutter.

This may seem an unlikely place for a church to be planted, but Paul decided to spend some time there. His visit occurred during what is called Paul's second missionary journey (around AD 49–52), and it is covered in Acts 15:40 – 18:22.

Paul's work in Corinth seems to have got off to a good start, and he met new friends – a married couple named Aquila and Priscilla. In a series of coincidences (better described perhaps as God-incidences), they discovered they had several things in common. All three were Jews by birth, had come to believe in Jesus of Nazareth as the Messiah and shared the same trade, being tent-makers They were linked by birth, new-birth and business!

Aquila and Priscilla had, along with other Jews, been expelled from Rome by decree of the emperor and had set up their trade in Corinth. It was usual for Jewish teachers (rabbis) to have a trade to support themselves. Tent-making probably covered working with all kinds of leather goods as well.

On meeting Paul, the couple took him into their home, and he joined them in their business. But his real purpose and passion was to talk about his discovery that Jesus of Nazareth was the long-promised Messiah, Yahweh's servant. Each Sabbath, Paul went to the local synagogue and used the opportunity to teach about Jesus, arousing considerable interest.

Two of Paul's team members, Silas and Timothy, joined him, which meant that they could act as breadwinners while Paul gave his full attention to preaching. The increasing number of converts that Paul was gaining led to controversy and abusive opposition in the synagogue. Paul, in a prophetic enactment, shook out his clothes as a symbolic act of his refusal to keep preaching to his fellow Jews. This practice of prophetic enactment was adopted by prophets in the Old Testament and was advocated by Jesus when he said, 'Shake the dust off your feet' (Matthew 10:14).

Now Paul concentrated exclusively on the non-Jewish population and made his point by setting up meetings in the house next door. One significant convert was the leader of the synagogue, Crispus, whom Paul baptized along with Crispus's entire household. This must have further inflamed those Jews who publicly opposed Paul – especially as news of Crispus's story probably encouraged other Corinthians to believe and be baptized.

On the surface, it would appear that Paul's time in Corinth was fruitful. Despite stiff opposition, people were coming to faith through him. The beginnings of a church plant were emerging. But it would seem that, deep within, Paul was facing a personal struggle. The battle was so intense that the Lord Jesus Christ appeared to him one night in a vision, with a strong message of assurance:

> Do not be afraid; keep on speaking, do not be silent. For I am with you, and no one is going to attack and harm you, because I have many people in this city.
> (Acts 18:9–10)

It seems that Paul was undergoing an intense personal crisis, which provoked a reaction of fear. The implication of the message from his risen Lord was that he was fearful enough to consider being silent and perhaps even leaving Corinth. We can't be sure of what caused Paul's fear, other than acknowledging that Corinth was spiritually a tough place to be. Like many cities in our modern world, there was probably a concentration of evil, with strong occult activities making it a dark place. Physically, Paul often endured the fury of the crowds, who rejected the message and beat the messenger as well. Only a few weeks before coming to Corinth, he had received a severe public flogging in Philippi and was likely still recovering from that ordeal. Jesus specifically assured Paul that he wouldn't be physically harmed in Corinth, and this gives a strong indication that part of his fear found its root here. Then there is the emotional pain that most of us experience when we are rejected. Long-term hostility and abuse take their toll on even the most resilient. Spiritually, physically and emotionally, Paul was under pressure. The words 'Do not be afraid' are better translated as an urgent command – 'Stop being afraid!' – suggesting that Paul was in a state of crisis.

We have privileged insight into what Paul faced as he wrote to the Corinthian congregation later on, which reveals something of his inner turmoil at this point in his life. More than that, he explains how he decided to deal with it. In 1 Corinthians 2:1–3, Paul writes with honesty about his inner struggle. He tells the Corinthian congregation that he came to Corinth 'in weakness with great fear and trembling' (1 Corinthians 2:3). Corinthians were conceited people, with an air of arrogance. They were proud of their wealth and saw themselves as intellectually superior to most. The city hosted the prestigious biannual Isthmian Games, and now out-shone the famed city of Athens as the capital of the province of Achaia. At one level, they had got it all. People who think that way about themselves are hard to reach with the gospel. There was much to make even a battle-hardened apostle feel weak at the knees.

Paul reveals his response to this challenge, which can be summarized as we consider his aim, attitude and actions.

Aim

Paul had made up his mind not to try to dazzle his audience with his skills of intellect and communication. Travelling speakers were two a penny in the first-century world, and many were professionally trained to impress by their oratory and presence. Paul didn't intend to travel that road. Instead, he made a steadfast resolution 'to know nothing while I was with you except Jesus Christ and him crucified' (1 Corinthians 2:2). He was determined to talk about Jesus and the climax of his mission, demonstrated by his death and resurrection. Paul understood that this was the heart of the good news which had the power to change people for good (Romans 1:16), and he determined that his sole aim would be to communicate that message for all he was worth.

Attitude

As we have already noted, Paul was not afraid to admit his vulnerability and use words like weakness, fear and trembling – hardly the kind of chapter headings we would find in a book about boosting your self-confidence! Perhaps this is best understood by reminding ourselves that Paul found that celebrating his weaknesses released in him a God-given strength. He writes about this profound lesson elsewhere (2 Corinthians 12:7–10; Philippians 4:10–13), and records his overwhelming sense of God-dependence in every area of his life. Paul was not a self-confident man. He knew that he had serious limitations. He was wholeheartedly God-dependent, as he knew divine resources would never run short.

Actions

Paul reminded his Corinthian congregation how he stayed true to his aim, relying on God's power rather than human eloquence (1 Corinthians 2:4–5). And people came to believe in Jesus as a result of the Holy Spirit's power in a way they could not have done through wise and persuasive words. Paul stayed true to his convictions, and through this, people were changed and a new community of believers was planted in one of the world's toughest cities.

If we look at the final verse of our reading from Acts 18, we read:

> So Paul stayed in Corinth for a year and a half, teaching them the word of God.
> (Acts 18:11)

Paul tended to be on the move most of the time, but he based himself in certain strategic centres for longer periods. Corinth was one such place; here he committed to eighteen months of preaching and teaching, which were probably a mixture of sharing the good news of Jesus with anyone who would listen and building up this young church in its new-found faith. But let's not see these eighteen months as merely a strategic decision. This was an act of both faith and courage. Jesus had told his servant Paul to stay put and keep speaking, to stop being afraid and to trust his promise that he wouldn't be attacked. He had said that there were many in that city who were God's people (even if they hadn't realized it yet!). Paul's decision to stay in Corinth was a personal victory over fear, and an example to us in our private struggles.

Learning from the story

What lessons can we draw from Paul's experience? Four things emerge from his honest account.

1. Fear is part of being human

It is strangely heartening to read that Paul battled with fear. We can sometimes run away with the unrealistic idea that the heroes and heroines of the Bible were somehow unmarked by the frailties we ourselves carry. But as we study their lives, we recognize that we share the same fault lines. Not all fears are unhealthy, either. For example, we bring up our children to have awareness of people and things that could potentially do harm. The Bible encourages us to fear God, and we need reverence, a healthy respect for him. So not all fear is bad, and it is part of the human condition.

2. There is strength in vulnerability

Paul is surprisingly up front in his admission of fear at facing Corinth, and this is linked to his determination to boast in his weaknesses. We would do well to meditate deeply on his insightful phrase: 'For when I am weak, then I am strong' (2 Corinthians 12:10). At the heart of this statement lay a real personal discovery for a man who possessed more talent than most: gifting, energy, ambition and the ability to inspire others are simply not enough. If we are going to be the best that we can be, then we need a strength that lies beyond ourselves. This is grace and it is God's gift to those who approach with humble hearts. Expressing our need and admitting that we don't have it all sewn up is a vital exercise in humility, which is, after all, a prime Christian virtue.[2]

This is not a licence for self-indulgence or seizing the opportunity to engage in an emotional striptease whenever we are asked, 'How are you?' I have been in church leadership long enough to know that some are skilled at hijacking any Christian meeting to run through a litany of their needs and wants. They are like the man who was told by his therapist, 'Stop wasting money on visiting me every week. Save the cash and take a trip to Niagara Falls. You just need to focus on something bigger than yourself!'

3. Face fear with a plan

There is little doubt that the vision of Jesus in the night helped Paul to reach a turning point at Corinth, and he probably replayed that promise many times in his head. He knew that he was where God wanted him to be. We can identify with the sense of security that this knowledge would have brought Paul. But as we have seen from his honest assessment of his aim, attitude and actions when facing Corinth, Paul had done some clear thinking as well. We too need to have strategies in place so that when fears arise, we have a script to follow. Going back to the story at the start of this chapter, following my scary roof experience, a friend (who happens to be a builder) asked if anyone had taught me to climb a ladder. I didn't come from a family where that kind of practical learning was on offer, so he spent an hour or two explaining the safety-first rules for handling heights. The lesson was valuable. Although it hasn't taken away my fear of heights, it has taught me how not to get stuck on a roof!

If we can identify what causes our feelings of fear (and we may need help to do this), then we can work out a plan of action to use when the need arises. Panic increases when we feel trapped and are confused about what to do, so it is wise to think and plan ahead.

4. Find strength in relationships

Corinth was hard soil in which to plant a church, and that must have affected Paul. It is worth noting that God arranged things so that Paul was not alone in this tough assignment. Aquila, Priscilla, Silas and Timothy all played their part in encouraging him in his work – even to the extent of providing the kind of practical support that makes life work better. Never underestimate the value of hospitality! Paul seems to have worked almost exclusively in team relationships, and there is a lesson here about the importance of partnership and the power of synergy.[3]

At the college where I teach, students are encouraged to form 'accountability partnerships' within the first few days of their undergraduate studies. This involves meeting with one or two friends on a weekly basis to share their lives and pray together. As we explain to them, this is a life skill that will help them survive and thrive in Christian leadership, and the sooner they get started the better.

Think about this sober assessment from Henri Nouwen:

> Much Christian leadership is exercised by people who do not know how to develop healthy, intimate relationships and have opted for power and control instead. Many Christian empire builders have been people unable to give and receive love.[4]

So what?

- Can you identify with Paul's experience in Corinth? What stands out most?
- Is fear always bad? For example, the Bible teaches that 'The fear of the LORD is the beginning of knowledge' and 'the beginning of wisdom' (Proverbs 1:7; 9:10). How can we separate healthy fears from unhealthy ones?
- How can vulnerability be expressed without becoming a 'look at me' exercise in self-indulgence?
- Can you think of practical ways in which you could develop a strategy for dealing with specific fears?
- How can we build mutually supportive relationships as followers of Jesus?

Maurice's story

Maurice Chevalier was a French actor and singer who made many Hollywood films and won fans worldwide.[5] At one point in his career, he suffered a serious breakdown, triggered by forgetting his lines during a stage performance in Paris. After a spell in hospital, he went to the South of France to recuperate. He lived with the terrifying memory of forgetting his lines and breaking down in front of a large audience, and vowed he would never perform in public again. It seemed that his career was over.

His local doctor was aware of this, but tried to persuade Maurice to perform one or two of his famous songs at the village fête. The doctor explained that the audience would number a few hundred and most would be friends and neighbours. Maurice steadfastly refused the invitation and would not even discuss it, making plain that even the thought of standing up in front of people caused deep emotional pain. The wise doctor uttered some words of advice that in later years, Maurice acknowledged, set him on the road to recovery in both health and career. 'Maurice,' the doctor said, 'don't be afraid to be afraid . . .'

These are wise words for those who believe that the absence of fear is the solution. It is not its absence that counts, but rather what we do when it is present. What Chevalier had to learn was how to deal with fear on the occasions it showed up – as we all do.

8. PETER AND IMPRISONMENT

Setting the scene

Rachel is a prisoner.

She has no release date to aim for and zero chance of parole.

Bereft of legal representation, Rachel has no hope of her situation ever being reviewed. Even the European Court of Human Rights won't touch her case.

Because Rachel is a prisoner of family love.

Brought up in a small town in the North of England, she grew up as an only child. After university she was recruited by a bank and moved to their head office in London. For the best part of twenty-five years, she commuted every weekday, braving the London rush hour. As a dutiful daughter, she made a few visits home each year, but in truth, her centre of gravity became her small flat above a grocer's shop in West London, and an engaging circle of friends.

Weekends were packed with activity. There was no shortage of things to do, places to visit and friends to entertain. There were a few boyfriends, but only one serious relationship that looked as if it could go the distance. Matt worked in the same office, and they shared an on-off romance that limped along for five or six years. Then he had the opportunity to transfer to the bank's New York office. When Matt accepted without asking how Rachel felt, she knew that they didn't have a shared future.

One morning she woke up and realized that she was middle-aged. She had a great job, good salary, nice pension and a large circle of married friends (most with families). Life was generally good – until circumstances changed.

Rachel's father had lost his sight a few years previously and was battling cancer. Her mother could have coped, but there were complications, which meant that Rachel had to leave her job and move back home to help. All their other family members were elderly and unwell, so it was down to her and her mum to nurse her dad until he died.

During the last few months of his life, Rachel's mum began to have issues with her own health. She now requires 24/7 care. Although they could probably afford a nursing home, Rachel had faithfully promised her mum that she would look after her for as long as she could. Her mum's greatest fear has been that of dying alone and 'somewhere strange'.

Rachel takes promises seriously. So her life now revolves around a routine of nursing, washing, cooking, cleaning and caring. A few visits to the supermarket are the highlight of her week, along with a couple of soaps, whose fantastic story-lines bring some colour to a monochrome life. She has occasional contact with a few old friends, but it's mainly Christmas and birthday cards. London is a long way.

Her mother now has dementia as well as her other health issues, so conversation is limited and increasingly distressing.

Rachel can't remember her last holiday, or even the last time she enjoyed a day to herself. She struggles to think beyond today. Life has stopped for her. And she has no clue if it will ever restart. If it does, what will it look like?

Prisons are places where hope often dies. There are a lot of prisoners like Rachel. Their prisons vary but they share the same condition. They are trapped not by walls but by circumstance.

Listening to the story – Acts 12:1–19

Our reading is set around ten years after the death and resurrection of Jesus. The community of his followers had grown significantly, and it hadn't gone unnoticed. Controversy was never far away from the first Christians, and the chapter opens with news of arrests. Included in the round-up was James, the brother of John, two of Jesus' closest companions.[1] Herod has James executed and notes how that boosts his poll ratings.

Herod (this was Agrippa I, grandson of Herod the Great) needed to keep both the Jews and the Romans on side, and this noisy sect who worshipped a king called Jesus provided an ideal opportunity. Former Bishop of Durham, Tom Wright, notes:

> It was strongly in his interests both to show his Roman overlords that he would not tolerate dangerous movements developing under his nose and to show his own people that he was standing up, as they would have seen it, for their ancestral traditions. To kill someone with the sword, as opposed to having them stoned as Stephen had been, strongly indicates that Herod either saw, or wanted people to think he saw, the Christian movement as a political threat.[2]

As a political move to boost his popularity further, Herod arrested Peter and placed him under armed guard with the intention of a public show trial once the feast of Passover had ended. Luke (who is keen on numbers) reveals the size of the military detail guarding a fisherman from Galilee.

He also records that the Christian community, on hearing this news, immediately turned to intense prayer, recognizing that they had nowhere to go, other than to God.[3]

We can only begin to imagine the sense of anxiety that pervaded the church. One key leader had been murdered, and Peter (under secure guard) was surely next. Jesus had prophesied that intense suffering faced his followers, and perhaps this was the time for Peter to face martyrdom. And what of Peter – what thoughts gripped his mind in the long night hours?

Astonishingly, on the eve of his trial, Peter slept soundly, despite being chained to two guards. Luke recounts an extra-ordinary series of events. An angel woke Peter none too gently, told him to get up, get dressed and follow him. We are not told what the armed guards were doing, but they seem to have been disabled in some way – possibly just asleep. Peter was led out of the prison and into the street, thinking at first that this was all a dream.

Perhaps it was the cold night air that helped Peter to realize that this wasn't a dream after all, but his next move was to go to where he was confident the church would gather: the home of Mary and her son John Mark.

There is something very funny about what happened next – although I have always felt sorry for the servant girl Rhoda, who has gone down in history as 'unwittingly, the comic star turn', when 'it is the church at prayer that ought to raise a smile at the same time'.[4]

Peter knocks on the door and identifies himself, and Rhoda, overcome with excitement, leaves him locked outside as she rushes in to interrupt the fervent praying with this amazing news. The faith-filled believers tell Rhoda that she is mad, although the more discerning among them try to find a more profound explanation . . . Peter's personal angel was putting in an appearance perhaps?[5] Meanwhile, a frozen apostle is still standing outside the front door, anxious to get off the street!

Eventually, he is let in, and an astonished group see a walking answer to their prayers. This was one prayer meeting that would never be forgotten! After spending a short time explaining all that had taken place, Peter removed himself to a place of safety, leaving behind a furious Herod, a palace full of puzzled people and some very worried guards.[6]

Learning from the story

But that was all back when extraordinary things were happening, as described in the Gospels and the book of Acts. What about now? How does Peter's experience help us to understand how to cope when we find ourselves trapped by circumstances beyond our control?

Peter's postcard from the edge contains several insights.

Mystery and miracles

We need to start with a question: why was James killed and Peter delivered? This only leads to other questions. Was it because James was less spiritual or more disposable? Did God like one more than the other? Didn't the church pray hard enough, or were their prayers lacking faith? Luke may have struggled with the same sorts of questions, but if he did, he doesn't mention them. But he places the different outcomes for two friends side by side: James is executed in prison, and Peter walks out a free man.

The different results can only be understood in the light of God's greater purpose, which we can't understand now but will one day. As Paul eloquently expressed it: 'For now we see only a reflection as in a mirror; then we shall see face to face. Now I know in part; then I shall know fully, even as I am fully known' (1 Corinthians 13:12).

There are any number of things that we know only in part, but trust that one day the questions will be answered. As a friend said as he mourned the death of his wife, 'I have become a reverent agnostic. I don't understand – but I do trust.'

Acts 12 mirrors the experience of real life. There are wonderful answers to prayer, and there are also prayers that go unanswered – or at least we don't get the answer we want. There are three possible answers to any prayer: 'yes', 'no' and 'wait'. We need to understand that 'no' is an acceptable answer to prayer.

As a pastor, I have experienced the tension of praying for someone to be healed (and fully believing that God has the power to heal), and then, several months later, conducting their funeral. I have wrestled, and still do, with the big questions that scream when tragedy strikes.

Chris Russell is a pastor too, and he has written about a tragedy that affected him deeply. His nephew, Tommy, was struck by a falling lamp post while asleep in his pushchair in a London street. Tommy was three days short of his first birthday. He died in hospital two days later. Chris wrote a letter to that nephew unveiling his grief, his questions, his faith – and above all, his hope. He rejects simplistic clichés about the accident being 'God's will' and ' "just" having to trust the sovereign God'. His letter to Tommy continues:

> Our faith must be able to have enough space in it for this event. Not to be made sense of – for that will never be – but simply to be an event that happened.

Nothing will ever be able to erase the sights and sounds, the smells and noises of those three days in the hospital. There we wept and groaned, we shook our heads in disbelief and we implored God to bring your life back from the brink.

I prayed every prayer I could think of, in every way I could think possible. I pleaded with God and bargained with him. I tried to convince him that he would get so much out of a miraculous healing now; imagine the lives that would be turned to him with such an intervention.

Our prayers weren't answered. We didn't get what we wanted. But what we did get was God's presence. There in the valley of the shadow of death, as we baptised you on the Tuesday night, as we prayed the following night, there came among us the divine man, a man of sorrows and one familiar with suffering . . .

This presence sometimes brings miraculous healing. Your death, Tommy, has not stopped me praying for that in others. But that is up to God, rather than to my technique or formula. Healing is the work of God's hands, but what we need most is his very presence, God's very self. And on his cross the world changes as God enters in.[7]

We need faith for the mysteries as well as the miracles.

Faith and faithfulness

You may have heard the answer given by a boy in Sunday school who was asked to define faith. He replied, 'Faith is believing things you know aren't true!' I think it's better to stick with the Bible's definition: 'Faith is the confidence that what we hope for will actually happen; it gives us assurance about things we cannot see' (Hebrews 11:1, NLT). We are also told that faith is not something we can somehow muster up from deep within ourselves. On the contrary, 'it is the gift of God' (Ephesians 2:8).

As mentioned earlier, faith is more than believing *in* God, it's more a case of *believing* God. From Peter's postcard, we can see a couple of strong examples of what that can look like. The church received the news of Peter's arrest with faith. They prayed with passion and withstood the temptation to flee, despite the likely fear that they were next on the list. And then there is Peter the night before his trial – so soundly asleep that the angelic visitor had to shake him awake! Sometimes faith calls us to action, and on other occasions it tells us to rest.

Faith is demonstrated when we are faithful in trusting, resting, believing and worshipping, especially in times of adversity. Have you noticed, in the book of Psalms, how the writers move almost seamlessly from reflecting on the need and state of the world to the praise of God? Take Psalm 36, for instance, where David begins with his indictment against those who are bent on evil and full of pride and lies, and then declares:

> Your love, LORD, reaches to the heavens,
>   your faithfulness to the skies.
> Your righteousness is like the highest mountains,
>   your justice like the great deep.
> (Psalm 36:5–6)

I used to struggle with the New Testament verse that tells us to 'give thanks in all circumstances' (1 Thessalonians 5:18). Then someone pointed out that we are not asked to thank God *for* everything that happens, but *in* all circumstances. The distinction is crucial. Peter was able to rest (literally!) even as he waited to face a hostile courtroom, and his friends were able to pray, believing in the ultimate power of a greater Judge.

Both responses show faith being exercised through faithful actions.

Pressure and perseverance

During the cold war, Christians across Eastern Europe faced considerable pressure because of their faith. I recall a conversation in the late 1970s with a leader who had been arrested and questioned on many occasions. He outlined a few recent incidents involving himself and others in his congregation, and told me that some church members were informants for the secret police. I did my best to offer words of support. But he cut me short: 'Read your New Testament, Ian! What we face here is normal according to the book!' He was absolutely right. Consider some sample passages:

In fact, everyone who wants to live a godly life in Christ Jesus will be persecuted. (2 Timothy 3:12)

Endure hardship as discipline; God is treating you as his children. (Hebrews 12:7)

Blessed are you when people insult you, persecute you and falsely say all kinds of evil against you because of me. Rejoice and be glad, because great is your reward in heaven, for in the same way they persecuted the prophets who were before you. (Matthew 5:11–12)

We must go through many hardships to enter the kingdom of God. (Acts 14:22)

Join with me in suffering, like a good soldier of Jesus Christ. (2 Timothy 2:3)

> Dear friends, do not be surprised at the fiery ordeal that has come on you to test you, as though something strange were happening to you. (1 Peter 4:12)

The pressure faced by followers of Jesus takes different forms. Acts 12 reminds us of those who suffer imprisonment and death for Jesus' sake. There are thousands in that situation even as you read these words. And just as the congregation in Jerusalem prayed fervently for Peter, so we should be going to God on behalf of those family members who suffer today.[8]

But as has already been noted, you don't have to be in a cell to feel imprisoned. So what is the faith response to pressure? How should we react to circumstances that hurt and won't go away? The New Testament gives a clear answer:

> Consider it a sheer gift, friends, when tests and challenges come at you from all sides. You know that under pressure, your faith-life is forced into the open and shows its true colors. So don't try to get out of anything prematurely. Let it do its work so you become mature and well-developed, not deficient in any way.
> (James 1:2–4, MSG)

Pressures are to be faced and seen as opportunities to grow in our faith and our relationship with God. I have lost count of the conversations with people who have been through some of the hardest trials that life throws up, but who have spoken of an enriching experience of finding God in the deep places. As I write these words, I recall a meal that my wife and I shared with a woman who had lived through her son's suicide and her husband's premature death. With tears, she told us, 'You never know Jesus is all you need, till Jesus is all you've got!'

At Moorlands College where I teach, we take our second-year students away on a residential training course called a Personal Development Exercise. Over several days, they face a mixture of challenges and tests, which they tackle in small teams. It is a fun atmosphere, with lots of healthy competition and some sudden surprises thrown in. The purpose of the exercise is to help students understand more about themselves and working well with others. And because we train Christian leaders, it helps us to consider where faith fits in, as well as seeing how to react well when under pressure.

We introduce the students to the '4 Ps'.[9] This chart explains the concept:

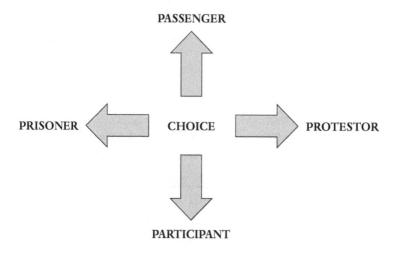

The different responses that these words represent are as follows.

Passenger
This is like someone sitting on a bus and looking out of the window at the surrounding countryside. They are not engaged

at all; they simply watch the world go by and allow circumstances to carry them to an unknown destination. They are spectating rather than getting involved.

Prisoner

This is the person who feels locked in, yet unable to do anything about it. They feel unheard and uncared for, and have a deep sense of injustice. Yet they keep quiet about their feelings. They are trapped.

Protester

This person won't keep quiet! They talk loud and long about what is wrong, and may even be able to identify what needs to happen to change the circumstances. But it is all talk and no action. And not everything that they argue about is rational or workable as a solution. It is more about letting off steam and having a moan.

Participant

This is the person who wants to engage in solving the situation, or at least in moving things forward towards a solution. They 'own' the responsibility of getting involved and are willing to become a 'change agent'.

The key word is at the centre of the diagram – choice. It invites the question: 'Which of these four positions do I choose to take in response to the circumstances that I face?'

So what?

- Do you feel imprisoned by circumstances? What are they?
- Is there anything in the Acts 12 passage that you find particularly helpful in your current situation?

- How can we find a balance between praying for miracles and living with mystery?
- Do you think we sometimes soft-pedal the pressures that come when someone chooses to follow Christ?
- Looking at the 4 Ps, which of the four options is your default setting?
- What is the most helpful thing we can do when we see someone else under pressure?

Debra's story

Debra Searle rowed across the Atlantic Ocean alone.[10]

It wasn't her original plan to row solo, but circumstances changed when her oarsman husband had to leave the 23-foot plywood boat, having developed an uncontrollable fear of the ocean.

Debra decided to go it alone, and a journey of 3,000 miles took her a gruelling three and a half months to complete. Battling against weather, massive waves and sharks, she rowed on for twelve hours every day. Three words became significant as she battled these challenges. Those words gave her focus, and Debra says they acted as a daily inspiration and corrective. Since making her epic voyage, she has become a highly acclaimed motivational speaker, addressing audiences around the world. She always repeats the three words that steered her to a momentous achievement: CHOOSE YOUR ATTITUDE.

We may not be able to change our circumstances, but we can make a choice about how we will respond to them. As people of faith, followers of Jesus are not immune to challenging situations that imprison them. We are called to walk by faith, not by sight. That means we trust in God's love and believe, whatever our circumstances, that he is in control.

That's why we can be so sure that every detail in our lives of love for God is worked into something good.

(Romans 8:28, MSG)

That's how prisoners become participants.

NOTES

1. Ruth and loss

1. Carolyn Custis James, *The Gospel of Ruth: Loving God Enough to Break the Rules* (Zondervan, 2008), p. 28.
2. Warren W. Wiersbe, *Put Your Life Together: Studies in the Book of Ruth* (Victor Books, 1985), pp. 9–12.
3. Custis James, *The Gospel of Ruth*, p. 42.
4. The purpose of 1:8–13 is to prepare the way for a turning point in the story. The custom in Israel was if a husband died, his brother or near relative was to marry the widow and preserve the brother's name (see Deuteronomy 25:5–10). Naomi refers to this custom in 1:11 when she declares that she has no other sons to marry Ruth and Orpah, so it is senseless for them to remain committed to her.
5. See Ruth 1:16–17 from the translation by Robert L. Hubbard Jr, *The Book of Ruth*, The New International Commentary on the Old Testament (Eerdmans, 1988), p. 114.
6. John Piper, *A Sweet and Bitter Providence: Sex, Race and Sovereignty in the Book of Ruth* (Inter-Varsity Press, 2010), pp. 60–61.

7. See Ruth 2:12, Hubbard's translation, *The Book of Ruth*, p. 153.

8. See, for example, Custis James, *The Gospel of Ruth*, pp. 144–155.

9. This tradition is helpfully explained by David Atkinson, *The Message of Ruth: The Wings of Refuge*, The Bible Speaks Today (Inter-Varsity Press, 1974), pp. 86–98.

10. Nigel G. Wright, *The Real Godsend: Preaching the Birth Narratives in Matthew and Luke* (BRF, 2009), pp. 22–23.

11. Steven Jeffers and Harold Smith, *Finding a Sacred Oasis in Grief* (Radcliffe Publishing, 2007).

12. One highly recommended book has been written by Dr Bill Merrington, *Grief, Loss and Pain in Churches: A Handbook for Understanding and Advising in a Christian Context* (Kevin Mayhew, 2011).

13. As quoted by Dale Ralph Davis, *The Message of Daniel: His Kingdom Cannot Fail*, The Bible Speaks Today (Inter-Varsity Press, 2013), p. 27.

14. Famously, the shortest verse in the Bible is John 11:35: 'Jesus wept.' Our Lord entered into the pain of grief felt by this family, even though he knew that he would shortly turn their mourning to dancing.

15. Source unknown.

16. For further information, see www.chsw.org.uk.

2. Elijah and despair

1. See Judges 2:10–15 for a description of how Israel forsook Yahweh and embraced Baal worship.

2. Dale Ralph Davis, *1 Kings: The Wisdom and the Folly* (Christian Focus, 2002), p. 233.

3. See 1 Kings 17:1–24, where we are told of the miraculous ways in which Elijah was protected and fed.

4. Elijah's challenge gets to the heart of the issue. Israel was trying to hold on to worship of both Yahweh and Baal (something called syncretism). The word 'waver' (v. 21) is the same word translated 'danced' in verse 26, and paints a picture of people hopping from one foot to another with indecision.

5. James emphasizes that Elijah's prayers were powerful and effective, but he sets this in context by saying that Elijah was human and we share that same humanity.

6. Some have speculated that Jezebel's intent was to strike fear in Elijah and cause him to flee. This was prompted by the apparent turn in public opinion. With Elijah gone, she would be able to rebuild the Baal cult unopposed. This would explain why she tips him off with a threat. Why send a messenger instead of an assassin?

7. Look at how the apostle Paul shows that behind dumb idols, demonic powers are at work (see 1 Corinthians 10:18–22).

8. Horeb is probably another name for Mount Sinai, where God revealed himself to Moses and gave the Ten Commandments (see Exodus 19:1ff.). This is located 200 miles south of Beersheba.

9. One of the prophecies relating to the coming of Jesus gives him the name Immanuel, which means 'God with us' (see Isaiah 7:14).

3. Esther and courage

1. Esther is the only book in the Bible that definitely doesn't mention God. Song of Songs may possibly also omit God's name, depending on how we translate 8:6.

2. Details can be found at www.bbc.co.uk/religion/religions/judaism/holydays/purim_1.shtml.

3. The Persian Empire lasted for 200 years from the sixth century BC. Xerxes I reigned for twenty years (486–465 BC).

4. This is the origin of the phrase, 'The law of the Medes and Persians', which refers to something that cannot be altered.

5. The guests were drunk (see v. 10), and at this stage things would probably have developed into more of an orgy than a sophisticated royal reception. Vashti's refusal is not surprising, given the circumstances.

6. History records that Xerxes suffered a series of military defeats against the Greeks between 482 and 479 BC, and it is likely that Esther 2:1 is placed at this time, when he was back at his palace licking his wounds.

7. This took place in 597 BC and was one of three mass deportations of Jews to Babylon. When Cyrus of Persia defeated the Babylonians, he decreed in 538 BC that the Jews were free to return to their homeland. But only 50,000 took up that offer. There is evidence that a large Jewish population remained.

8. The book uses her Persian name, Esther, which means 'star'. But when introducing her, the writer gives her Hebrew name, Hadassah, meaning 'myrtle'.

9. It is likely that Mordecai gave this advice because of some prevailing anti-Semitism. Life in the harem would have meant that Esther couldn't observe kosher food laws, and this may have been another factor.

10. From an article by Simon Rocker (Judaism Editor of the *Jewish Chronicle*), 'Judaism Lets Its Hair Down', *The Times*, 18 March 2000.

11. See 1 Samuel 15:1, where Saul forfeits the throne for his disobedience in sparing Agag's life. For a helpful explanation of the case connecting Haman to this historic conflict, see Debra Reid's excellent book, *Esther*, Tyndale Old Testament Commentaries (Inter-Varsity Press, 2008), pp. 88–91.

12. The Persian word for 'lot' (dice) was *pur* – the origin of the word *Purim* as a Jewish festival.

13. The Greek historian Herodotus records that anyone approaching the Persian king unsummoned would be killed, unless the king gave an immediate pardon. (Herodotus 3.118, 140).

14. See Reid, *Esther*, for a translation of the Greek text, which gives a memorably dramatic description of Esther's approach to the king (pp. 165–166).

15. See www.history.ucsb.edu/faculty/marcuse/projects/niem/StuttgartDeclaration.htm.

16. This appears in various versions, as Niemöller adapted and used it in different contexts. This is the official version, according to the Martin Niemöller Foundation. See www.martin-niemoeller-stiftung.de/4/daszitat/a31.

17. http://lens.blogs.nytimes.com/2009/06/03/behind-the-scenes-tank-man-of-tiananmen/?_r=0.

18. It would appear that the origin of this quotation is the Jewish theologian Hillel, one of the most influential scholars in Jewish history: 'If I am not for myself, then who will be for me? And if I am only for myself, then what am I? And if not now, when?', www.jewishvirtuallibrary.org/jsource/Quote/hillel2.html.

19. Ian Coffey, *Working It Out: God, You and the Work You Do* (Inter-Varsity Press, 2008), p. 48.

20. www.independent.co.uk/news/world/asia/the-full-text-malala-yousafzai-delivers-defiant-riposte-to-taliban-militants-with-speech-to-the-un-general-assembly-8706606.html.

4. Jeremiah and inadequacy

1. Part of the famous ceiling in the Sistine Chapel, Rome and dated around 1512. See http://sistinepuzzle.com/the-weeping-prophet.

2. One of Rembrandt's earliest works, dated around 1630. See www.rembrandtpainting.net/rmbrndt_1620-35/jeremiah.htm.

3. See Jeremiah 27:6–7, where Jeremiah describes Nebuchadnezzar, king of the Babylonians, as Yahweh's 'servant'.

4. Manasseh (697–642 BC), Amon (642–640 BC), Josiah (640–609 BC), Jehoahaz (609 BC), Jehoiakim (609–598), Jehoiachin (598–597 BC) and Zedekiah (597–586 BC). Jeremiah probably began his public preaching during the reign of Josiah and continued until 585 BC. We have no record of how and where he died, but Jewish tradition maintains that he was stoned to death while living in Egypt (see Hebrews 11:37).

5. Josiah came to the throne at the tender age of eight, and he reigned for thirty-one years. He was a good king who won Jeremiah's approval (see Jeremiah 22:15–16), but he was also the last godly king to reign before the exile. See 2 Kings 22:1ff.

6. This is the title of Eugene Peterson's book on the Psalms of Ascent, taken from a quote by Friedrich Nietzsche (1844–1900). E. Peterson, *A Long Obedience in the Same Direction: Discipleship in an Instant Society* (Marshall Pickering, 1980).

7. In 605 BC, the Babylonians took captive some of the most able people of Judah (including Daniel and his friends); in 597 BC, thousands more were exiled. In 587 BC, Jerusalem was sacked and Solomon's magnificent temple destroyed. This devastating event 'must have seemed to be the death not just of a city but of an entire nation' – Simon Sebag Montefiore, *Jerusalem: The Biography* (Weidenfeld & Nicolson, 2011), p. 44.

8. William J. Petersen, *Jeremiah: The Prophet Who Wouldn't Quit* (Masthof Press, 2008).

9. Eugene Peterson, *Run with the Horses: The Quest for Life at Its Best* (InterVarsity Press, 1983), p. 203.

10. J. R. R. Tolkien, *The Fellowship of the Ring* (HarperCollins, 1997), p. 61.

11. Ian Stackhouse, *Primitive Piety: A Journey from Suburban Mediocrity to Passionate Christianity* (Paternoster, 2012), p. 128.

5. John the Baptist and doubt

1. It is worth reading the details of John's life that we find in all four Gospels, which include the remarkable circumstances surrounding his birth. See Matthew 3:1–17; 14:1–12; Mark 1:1–8; Luke 1:57–80; 3:1–20; John 1:19–34; 3:22–30.
2. Herodias was married to his brother Philip. As well as being Herod Antipas' sister-in-law, she was also his niece. John openly preached against this behaviour as being contrary to God's law (see Leviticus 18:16; 20:21).
3. F. B. Meyer, *John the Baptist* (Marshall, Morgan & Scott, 1954), p. 113.
4. Daniel Meyer, *Witness Essentials* (InterVarsity Press, 2012), pp. 32–33.
5. See Isaiah 40:3. All four Gospel writers link this verse from Isaiah directly to John the Baptist: Matthew 3:3; Mark 1:3; Luke 3:4; and John 1:23.
6. Jesus applied this passage to himself when he spoke at the synagogue in his home village of Nazareth. He did this at the start of his public ministry as a declaration of intent. As a result, it is often referred to as the 'Nazareth Manifesto'.
7. Repentance is not a familiar word, and this can lead to confusion. It means to change your mind and then your direction. It is more than saying sorry.
8. Beatitude simply means 'blessed'. There are forty-five listed in the Old Testament and forty-four in the New Testament. Luke and Matthew group some of Jesus' beatitudes together (Matthew 5:2–12; Luke 6:20–26). The fact that the lists are not identical suggests that Jesus may have repeated them at different times to separate audiences. Matthew includes eight

beatitudes at the beginning of Jesus' famous Sermon on the Mount.

9. William Barclay, *The Gospel of Luke*, The Daily Study Bible, 3rd edn (Saint Andrew Press, 1956), p. 89.

6. John Mark and failure

1. Ian Coffey, *21st Century Christian Magazine*, December 1988.

2. Gordon MacDonald, *Rebuilding Your Broken World* (Thomas Nelson, 1988).

3. Ibid., p. 16.

4. See Acts 12:25, where Barnabas and Saul visited Jerusalem with a financial gift to help the church (see Acts 11:27–30 for more details). We are told that John Mark and Barnabas were cousins in Colossians 4:10.

5. See Acts 13:3 – although John Mark is not mentioned by name, we can infer his presence, because his withdrawal from the team is specifically mentioned by Luke shortly afterwards (see Acts 13:13).

6. See Acts 4:36–37, where Barnabas is first mentioned. We discover that his real name was Joseph and that he was a Jew. Barnabas was a nickname given by the leaders of the Jerusalem church. It means 'son of encouragement', which says much about him.

7. Paul was the apostolic name by which he became known. Luke records the power encounter at Paphos as the defining moment when the balance of power shifted. Barnabas had nurtured Paul, having seen his potential from the earliest days. Paul was small enough to let this happen (see Acts 9:26–30; 11:25–26).

8. What has become known as Paul's first missionary journey was around AD 46–48, and the second one took place *c.* AD 49–52.

9. The Greek word translated as 'a sharp disagreement' (Acts 15:39) is *paraxysmos*, from which we derive the word 'paroxysm'. 'When the word is used in a medical context it can mean "convulsion" or refer to someone running a high fever. It carries overtones of severely heightened emotions, red and distorted faces, loud voices, things that were better left unsaid. A sorry sight' – Tom Wright, *Acts for Everyone: Part 2* (SPCK, 2008), p. 53.

10. For those who struggle with this dispute between friends, it is worth reminding ourselves that even the best leaders share our fallen human nature. But God can overrule. 'Sometimes disagreements among Christians seem intractable because they arise from differences of experience, insight or character. In this case the partners disagreed about the wisdom of taking a colleague on a long and arduous journey, with a small team requiring unanimity, trust and mutual support, when the person himself had previously proved to be unreliable in the course of a similar undertaking . . . Luke does not pass judgement on either party, but indicates that good came out of the separation, because two mission teams were formed' – David G. Peterson, *The Acts of the Apostles*, Pillar New Testament Commentaries (Eerdmans, 2009), p. 448.

7. Paul and fear

1. Adapted from J. Oswald Sanders, *Men from God's School* (Marshall, Morgan & Scott, 1965), p. 198.

2. See Jesus' teaching on this topic: Matthew 5:3–5; 18:1–4; Luke 14:11.

3. Synergy is the working together of two or more things (muscles or drugs, for example) to produce a result greater than the sum of their individual effects. It is a primary value of teamwork.

4. Henri J. M. Nouwen, *In the Name of Jesus* (Crossroad, 1989), p. 60.

5. Maurice Chevalier (1888–1972); the origin of this story is unknown.

8. Peter and imprisonment

1. Jesus nicknamed the pair 'sons of thunder', which was probably a lighthearted reference to their tendency to get angry (see Mark 3:17; Luke 9:54–55). With Peter, they formed an inner cabinet among the disciples and shared in significant moments such as the Transfiguration (see Luke 9:28–36).

2. Tom Wright, *Acts for Everyone: Part 1* (SPCK, 2008), p. 182.

3. Luke uses an adverb that denotes that the prayer was fervent and unremitting. He uses the same word in his Gospel to describes Jesus' intense praying in Gethsemane (see Luke 22:44).

4. Wright, *Acts for Everyone: Part 2* (p. 185).

5. This reflects the view that everyone has a personal angel (sometimes termed 'guardian angels' – see Matthew 18:10; Hebrews 1:14), and that they resemble the person for whom they care.

6. The conclusion of the chapter details Herod's sudden death. Luke's literary purpose in including this is seen in Acts 12:24: 'But the word of God continued to spread and flourish.' In other words, even a powerful tyrant can't thwart God's purpose. For some interesting background on this final section, see John R. W. Stott, *The Message of Acts: To the Ends of the Earth*, The Bible Speaks Today (Inter-Varsity Press, 1990), pp. 212–213.

7. Chris Russell, *To Be Delivered in the Event of My Death: Ten Letters* (Darton, Longman & Todd, 2012), pp. 117, 119.

8. Open Doors is one of several organizations that mobilize prayer and practical support for those persecuted for their faith. Their World Watch list currently has fifty countries where faith costs the most. They report that persecution has increased in recent years. See www.opendoors.uk.org.

9. Source unknown.

10. Debra Searle (MBE) wrote about her voyage under her previous name, Debra Veal, *Rowing It Alone: One Woman's Extraordinary Transatlantic Adventure* (Robson Books, 2003). She subsequently wrote a second book dealing with the techniques that kept her motivated on the voyage, which was published as Debra Searle, *The Journey: How to Achieve against the Odds* (Shoal Projects, 2007). See www.debrasearle.com.

also by Ian Coffey

Housegroups
The leader's survival guide
Ian Coffey &
Stephen Gaukroger (eds.)

ISBN: 978-1-84474-510-4
192 pages, paperback

Ideas, resources and encouragement for small-group leaders.

Ever since New Testament times small groups of Christians have met to learn, to worship and to grow together. An effective group enables its members to thrive in their Christian life and make an impact in their world.

This guide equips small-group leaders to steer a group with confidence and competence. Written by experienced authors with much wisdom, it will give you the vision you are looking for.

Essential reading whether you're starting a housegroup, taking an existing group forward or revitalizing a group that has gone a little flat, this practical guide will transform your vision, develop your skills, focus your aims and enable you to lead your group with panache.

'Wise, biblical and down-to-earth advice, often laced with humour, by those who have been there, done it and got the housegroup!' Steve Brady

Available from your local Christian bookshop or **www.thinkivp.com**

also by Ian Coffey

FAITH AT WORK SERIES

Working It Out
God, you and the work you do
Ian Coffey

ISBN: 978-1-84474-219-6
192 pages, paperback

Can welding a gatepost bring glory to God? Does ironing your children's uniforms help you grow as a disciple? Will your new crime prevention strategy do anything to further the kingdom?

To all three Ian Coffey says a resounding 'yes'. With lively Bible teaching and drawing on a wealth of real-life stories, he shows how work was part of God's good plan for men and women – given to us so we can make a creative contribution in his world.

Whatever your work, God is interested in it, God can transform it, and God wants to use it – for his glory.

'Whether we are a tinker, tailor, soldier, sailor or candlestick-maker – lawyer, church leader, office worker, stay-at-home mum or dad – this book can not only transform the way we look at our work, but also helps us understand how God sees it.' Rob Parsons

Available from your local Christian bookshop or **www.thinkivp.com**

Storytelling
*Sharing the gospel with
passion and power*
Martin Goldsmith

ISBN: 978-1-78359-155-8
192 pages, paperback

Martin Goldsmith discovered early in his career as a missionary
that stories were the most effective way of sharing the gospel
– especially in places where evangelism was illegal. But, since
then, he's discovered that they are also often the best way of
sharing it with our neighbours in the West, who are suspicious of
religious truth and hate being preached at.

Full of colourful stories from a lifetime of sharing the gospel, this
book shows us how to do the same. The author demonstrates
how the Bible teaches its theology through story, and how
other faiths are shaped by their storytelling – giving us a deeper
understanding of how we can reach others and teach real and
significant truths in an enthralling way.

If we want to win hearers for the gospel in today's world, it is
vital to become compelling and persuasive tellers of the gospel
story once again.

*'A must-read for those concerned to share the Greatest Story
Ever Told. From a wealth of experience, Martin Goldsmith shares
some riches about the power of storytelling.'* Ian Coffey

Available from your local Christian bookshop or **www.thinkivp.com**

For more information about IVP
and our publications visit
www.ivpbooks.com

Get regular updates at **ivpbooks.com/signup**
Find us on **facebook.com/ivpbooks**
Follow us on **twitter.com/ivpbookcentre**

Inter-Varsity Press, a company limited by guarantee registered in England and Wales, number 05202650. Registered office IVP Bookcentre, Norton Street, Nottingham NG7 3HR, United Kingdom. Registered charity number 1105757.